# Acknowledgments

I am grateful to several people at Bedford/St. Martin's who were actively involved in the book's development and production. Bedford founder and former president Charles Christensen and current president Joan Feinberg helped us plan the book. Developmental editor Michelle Clark responded to the manuscript, offering intelligent suggestions and upbeat encouragement. Book editor Anne Noonan guided our complex manuscript expertly through production.

Thanks also go to Claire Seng-Niemoeller for designing the book's pages and to copyeditor Barbara Flanagan for bringing consistency and clarity to the final manuscript.

Finally, since Diana Hacker will always be a part of my work on the exercises, I'd like to echo her words: "For their support and encouragement, we would like to thank our families, our colleagues at Prince George's Community College, and the many students over the years who have taught us that errors, a natural by-product of the writing process, are simply problems waiting to be solved."

Wanda Van Goor
Prince George's Community College

# Introduction for Students

To learn any skill—whether snowboarding, tennis, chess, CPR, HTML coding, or the electric guitar—takes practice. Writing well is no exception: In a college composition class, you will learn to write by writing, and you will learn to revise by revising.

*Developmental Exercises to Accompany RULES FOR WRITERS* will sharpen your revision skills by giving you a great deal of controlled, yet realistic, practice. Let's say, for example, that you want to learn to identify and revise sentence fragments. Your first step is to read section 19 in *Rules for Writers,* Sixth Edition, and to study the flow chart on page 149. Then, keeping *Rules for Writers* open to section 19, work on Exercise 19-1 in *Developmental Exercises to Accompany RULES FOR WRITERS.* Exercise 19-1, which we call a "guided practice," gives codes in the margin (such as 19a or 19c) next to all fragments. In addition to alerting you where to look for fragments, the codes refer to specific rules in the text, so if you have trouble identifying or fixing a particular fragment, you can consult *Rules for Writers* for help. When you have finished the exercise, you should check your answers. Answers to the first exercise in each set appear in the back of this book, beginning on page 185.

Once you have done the guided practice exercise, attempt the other exercises in the set; continue to refer to *Rules for Writers* when you run into trouble. You'll find that the rest of the exercises in a set vary in style and level of difficulty. In the set on fragments, for example, one exercise asks you to identify the complete sentence in a pair of word groups; another, presented in paragraph form, asks you to identify fragments and to think about possible revision strategies; and four other exercises give you practice in both identifying and revising fragments. Throughout the entire set, the subject you'll be reading about is the Beatles. Other exercise sets resemble the one on fragments. In those sets you will encounter a number of famous people you are likely to read about in other college classes: men and women such as Karl Marx, Harriet Beecher Stowe, Frederick Douglass, Albert Einstein, Aesop, and Amelia Earhart.

**Wanda Van Goor**
Prince George's Community College

*Developmental Exercises to Accompany*

# RULES FOR WRITERS

*Sixth Edition*

Wanda Van Goor

*Prince George's Community College*

Diana Hacker

*Bedford / St. Martin's*    Boston ◆ New York

Manufactured in the United States of America.

2   1   0   9   8   7
f   e   d   c   b   a

*For information, write:* Bedford/St. Martin's,
75 Arlington Street, Boston, MA 02116
(617) 399-4000

ISBN-10: 0–312–47279–X
ISBN-13: 978–0–312–47279–5

# Preface for Instructors

The exercises in this book are specifically designed for developmental students. A few are new, and all have been classroom tested.

The exercises in each set are thematically linked, usually focusing on the achievements of a famous person or group—such as Harriet Beecher Stowe, Frederick Douglass, Aesop, Amelia Earhart, Jackie Robinson, or the Beatles—so that students are reading real prose on interesting topics rather than unrelated drill sentences.

Here are the principal features of *Developmental Exercises to Accompany RULES FOR WRITERS,* Sixth Edition.

### Respectful of the student's college status

Although the exercises vary in level of difficulty, all of them respect the age and experience of college students; none insults their intelligence. Most exercises ask students to edit paragraphs and essays, not to fill in blanks or recopy whole sentences when only a word or two may need changing. Where possible, exercises encourage students to think about the impact of errors on readers and to choose revision strategies that produce effective, not just "correct," writing.

### Written in connected discourse

Because nearly every exercise is a paragraph, an essay, or a set of numbered sentences that are connected in meaning, students learn to identify and revise problem sentences in realistic contexts. These connected discourse exercises mimic the process of revision as it occurs in real life. In addition, they provide a rhetorical context to guide students as they choose one revision strategy over another. When revising comma splices and fused sentences, for example, students will see that relying too heavily on the period and the semicolon results in dull, monotonous prose. They will begin to see the need for occasional subordination, and the rhetorical context will suggest just where subordination would be most effective.

### "Guided practice" exercises

Most sections open with a guided practice exercise that gives students special help. Section codes (such as 8a, 8b) in the margin identify problem sentences and tell students where in *Rules for Writers,* Sixth Edition, to look for explanations and revision strategies. Answers to these exercises appear in the back of the book.

### Varied formats

Seldom will students be asked to do exactly the same thing in two adjacent exercises. Varied ways of working on a topic keep the task interesting. Sometimes students need only to circle the letter of the correct or clearer sentence in a pair of sentences; sometimes they choose between two words or phrases; frequently they edit, crossing out incorrect or confusing forms and adding handwritten revisions; occasionally they edit the same sentence in two different ways.

Many exercises provide hints for students, telling them, for example, that two of the ten sentences in a set are correct or that half of the sentences use a strategy, such as parallelism, correctly and the other half need revision.

### Emphasis on reading

As they learn to edit the paragraphs and essays in the exercises, students do a considerable amount of reading, and many exercises ask them to respond as readers. In an exercise on mixed constructions, for example, students are asked to discriminate between the easy-to-read and the hard-to-read sentences. Where possible, students are encouraged to think about meaning. "Which sentences are ambiguous?" asks an exercise on needed words. "What is the difference in meaning between the sentences 'Most slaves did not find their escape routes easy' and 'Most slaves did not find their escape routes easily'?" asks an exercise on adjectives and adverbs.

### Cross-curricular content

Most exercises profile a person or group that students are likely to encounter in college courses across the curriculum: Mary Wollstonecraft, Albert Einstein, Martin Luther King Jr., Louis Braille, Mother Jones, and so on. Because many of these people overcame great obstacles to achieve their goals, their stories are often inspirational as well as informative.

### Adaptable to a variety of teaching styles

You can use the exercises in a variety of ways. We have used them successfully for homework or quizzes, for nongraded individual study, for class discussions, and for collaborative learning in small groups.

# Contents

## Clarity (word choice)

## Grammar

## ESL challenges

## Punctuation

## Mechanics

## Basics

## EXERCISE 8-1    Active verbs: Guided practice

Revise any weak or unemphatic sentences by replacing passive verbs or *be* verbs with active alternatives. The numbers in the margin refer to appropriate revision strategies in section 8 of *Rules for Writers*, Sixth Edition. The first revision has been done for you, and a suggested revision of this exercise appears in the back of the book.

*Young slave Frederick Douglass enjoyed indulging*

~~Indulging~~ in his favorite fantasy about slave owners.~~was something that young~~    *8b*

~~slave Frederick Douglass enjoyed.~~ In his fantasy, everyone was in a conspiracy    *8b*

against the slave owners. No hint of an impending escape was given by slaves still    *8a*

in bondage. Members of the community never revealed the whereabouts of escaped

slaves. Slaves who escaped successfully never talked too much about how they got

away. Owners were told nothing at all by slaves they recaptured. Even some white    *8a*

southerners who sympathized with the slaves gave no information to their slave-

owning friends. The part of his fantasy that Douglass enjoyed the most was the fi-    *8b*

nal part. In it, Douglass imagined slave owners as being too afraid to hunt escaping    *8b*

slaves. The owners were distrustful of their slaves, their enemies, and even their

friends.

## EXERCISE 8-2     Active verbs     To read about this topic, see section 8 in *Rules for Writers*, Sixth Edition.

In the paired sentences below, circle the letter of the sentence that makes better use of its verbs. Be ready to explain your choice. Example:

   a. On his second attempt, Frederick was able to escape by pretending to be a sailor.

   (b.) On his second attempt, Frederick escaped slavery by pretending to be a sailor.

1a. The use of another man's sailing papers was the way Frederick got as far as Philadelphia.

 b. Frederick used another man's sailing papers to get as far as Philadelphia.

2a. He did not even consider the possibility of staying in Philadelphia.

 b. The possibility of staying in Philadelphia was not even considered by him.

3a. In Philadelphia, he asked the first black man he saw how to get to New York.

 b. In Philadelphia, the first black man he saw was asked how to get to New York.

4a. Arriving in New York was what made Frederick feel safe.

 b. Arriving in New York made Frederick feel safe.

5a. Luckily, a sympathetic abolitionist found Frederick before a slave catcher could find him.

 b. Luckily, Frederick was found by a sympathetic abolitionist before a slave catcher could find him.

**EXERCISE 8-3    Active verbs**    To read about this topic, see section 8 in *Rules for Writers*, Sixth Edition.

Half of the following sentences contain passive verbs or verbs that are a form of *be*. Find them and change them to active verbs. You may need to invent a subject for some verbs, and you may need to make major revisions in some sentences. If a sentence already contains only active verbs, mark it "active." Example:

*P*                                   *annoyed Frederick Douglass.*

~~Frederick Douglass was annoyed by~~ people who spoke openly of helping on the underground railroad/
                                                                                    ^

1. Douglass said that by talking openly about it, these people had turned the "underground railroad" into an "upperground railroad."

2. Although these people were deserving of praise, their open talk endangered escaping slaves.

3. Such talk alerted slave owners to possible escape routes.

4. Escaping slaves would often be caught by professional slave hunters at the houses of those who talked openly.

5. All slaves were threatened by any information that increased the slave owners' knowledge.

6. Whenever slave owners suspected some of the escape routes, the courage of the slaves was lost.

7. Frederick Douglass understood the slaves' fears very well; his first attempt to escape had failed.

8. Professional slave breakers beat and tortured runaway slaves until the slaves submitted or died.

9. His own treatment at the hands of slave breakers left Douglass with severe, disfiguring scars all over his back.

10. Years later, northerners were convinced by those scars that Douglass spoke the truth about slavery.

## EXERCISE 8-4    Active verbs: Guided review

Revise any weak or unemphatic sentences by replacing passive verbs or *be* verbs with active alternatives. The numbers in the margin refer to appropriate revision strategies in section 8 of *Rules for Writers,* Sixth Edition. The first revision has been done for you.

*changed some of his*

~~Some of~~ Frederick Douglass's ideas about the North ~~were changed~~ after his         *8a*
successful escape from slavery. Before that time, Douglass's assumption was that         *8b*
northerners lacked both money and culture. In the South, only poor people owned
no slaves. Also, no lovely homes, no pianos, no art, and often no books were owned         *8a*
by poor people. When he first saw New Bedford, Massachusetts, Douglass was         *8b*
doubtful of his own eyesight. He saw no dilapidated houses or naked children or
barefoot women in New Bedford. Instead, the beautiful homes with equally beautiful furniture and gardens were an indication of considerable wealth.  Quality mer-         *8b*
chandise was handled by laborers on the wharves and purchased by them in the         *8a*
stores. When he saw all of this, Douglass happily changed his ideas about the North.

## EXERCISE 9-1    Parallelism: Guided practice

Edit the following paragraphs to correct faulty parallelism. The numbers in the margin refer to appropriate rules in section 9 of *Rules for Writers*, Sixth Edition. The first revision has been done for you, and a suggested revision of this exercise appears in the back of the book.

In his own time, one famous sixteenth-century man was known only by his given name, "Leonardo." Today he is still known by that single name. But then and now, that name suggests many different roles for its owner: biologist, botanist, inventor, engineer, strategist, researcher, and artist.

Sixteenth-century Venetian soldiers knew Leonardo as a military strategist. When the Turkish fleet was invading their country, Leonardo suggested conducting surprise underwater attacks and ~~to flood~~ *flooding* the land that the Turkish army had to cross. Engineers knew him as the man who laid out new canals for the city of Milan. Scientists admired him for not only his precise anatomical drawings but also for his discovery that hardening of the arteries could cause death. To Milan's royal court, Leonardo was the artist who was painting impressive portraits, sculpting a bronze horse memorial to the house of Sforza, and at the same time worked on a mural of the Last Supper. *9b*

*9b*

*9a*

Leonardo saw a three-dimensional *s*-curve in all of nature—the flow of water, the movements of animals, and how birds flew. We recognize the same *s*-curve today in the spiraling form of DNA. Leonardo invented the wave theory: He saw that grain bending as the wind blew over it and water rippling from a stone cast into it were the same scientific event. It was as easy for him to see this wave in sound and light as observing it in fields and streams. The math of his day could not explain all his theories, but twentieth-century scientists showed the world that Leonardo knew what he was talking about. *9a*

*9b*

Leonardo saw very clearly that the powers of nature could be destructive and human beings could be savage. At the same time, he saw a unity holding all life's varied parts together, a unity he could express in his art. *9c*

"Leonardo"—it's quite a name!

## EXERCISE 9-2    Parallelism    To read about this topic, see section 9 in *Rules for Writers*, Sixth Edition.

All of the following sentences make an attempt to use parallel structure. Half of them succeed. The other five need revision. Put "OK" by the correct ones, and edit the other five to correct faulty parallelism. Example:

> Leonardo spent the first years of his life playing in the fields, drawing animals and plants, and
> *building*
> ~~he built~~ miniature bridges and towers along the river.
> ʌ

1. When Leonardo moved to Florence to live with his father, he exchanged a slow-moving rural life for a fast-paced urban one.

2. Because his birth parents had not been married, many job opportunities were not available to Leonardo. He could not become a merchant, a banker, or a skilled craftsman.

3. It was no easier for Leonardo to attend the local university than learning a craft.

4. The obvious choices were to become a soldier or he could join the priesthood.

5. Leonardo did not want his future to be in either the church or the army.

6. Deciding that Leonardo could draw better than he could march or pray, his father placed him with a major artist, Andrea del Verrocchio.

7. Verrocchio's shop did work for all kinds of customers, including trade unions, churches, and they would do work for individuals also.

8. Living in Verrocchio's home and working in his shop, Leonardo heard talk of new theories about geography and science while he learned skills like modeling, painting, and sculpture.

9. Perhaps even more important was the variety of instruments Leonardo learned to make, among them musical, navigational, and ones for surgeons to use.

10. Working with Verrocchio was like going to three schools: an art school, a technology institute, and a liberal arts college.

## EXERCISE 9-3    Parallelism    To read about this topic, see section 9 in *Rules for Writers*, Sixth Edition.

Circle the letter of the word or word group that best completes the parallel structure in each sentence. Example:

>    Leonardo was handsome, generous, clever, and _____.
>
>    (a.) ambidextrous
>
>    b. able to use either hand for most activities
>
>    c. he could use either hand for most activities

1. Leonardo's life had three distinct periods: his childhood in Vinci, his apprenticeship in Florence, and _____.
   a.  when he was an adult
   b.  his being an adult and earning his own way
   c.  his adulthood in various Italian cities

2. In childhood, Leonardo had not only a loving family and relatives but also _____.
   a.  safe and unspoiled acres to explore
   b.  he had the whole gentle slope of a mountain to explore
   c.  including fields and vineyards to explore

3. However, two natural events haunted his memory for years: a hurricane destroyed much of the valley below his village, and _____.
   a.  a flood washed away much of the city of Florence
   b.  a flood that washed away much of the city of Florence
   c.  the boiling, muddy, surging waters of a flood

4. Wind and water became major topics for Leonardo's study. He decided that wind and water were both useful and _____.
   a.  did harmful things
   b.  they caused harm
   c.  harmful

5. Viewers can find in many of Leonardo's works small round pebbles washed by a stream, riverbanks covered with moss and flowers, and _____.
   a.  little freshwater crabs partly hidden beneath rocks
   b.  viewers can find small freshwater crabs under rocks
   c.  little freshwater crabs sometimes hide beneath rocks

## EXERCISE 9-4    Parallelism: Guided review

Edit the following paragraphs to correct faulty parallelism. The numbers in the margin refer to appropriate rules in section 9 of *Rules for Writers,* Sixth Edition. The first revision has been done for you.

Leonardo's vision of life as one borderless unity affected both his personal life

and ~~it affected~~ his artistic work.                                                                        9b

Leonardo did not simply look at the world; he studied it carefully. Watching the

wind ripple the water in a pond, he was observant, intent, and in a serious mood.        9a

Leonardo saw no boundaries in nature; to him, people and animals were parts of one

creation. He ate no meat because he did not want to bring death to a fellow creature;

he bought caged songbirds so that he could set them free. Having no family of his

own, he adopted a boy from another family to be both his son and he would be his        9b

heir. Even right- and left-handedness were the same to him. He filled his notebooks

with mirror writing, but he wrote letters, reports, and proposals in the usual way.

When his right hand became crippled, he used his left.

Leonardo's view of all of life as one creation led him to artistic innovations.

Before Leonardo, artists had always used outlines to separate a painting's subject

from its background. Because Leonardo saw everything in nature as interrelated, he

decided that using shadow and gradation of light and color was better than to use        9b

an outline. He wanted one thing to flow into another the way smoke flows into air.

Looking at Mona Lisa's hand, for instance, viewers can find no line where one finger

ends and the next one begins; the separation is done totally with shadows. This uni-

fied vision of the world affected the content of his paintings as well as the technique.

Background and subject often echo each other in a picture: The drapery and folds

of the subject's clothing may reflect background scenes of curving vines or rocky

hills or water that flows.                                                                                        9a

Leonardo recognized the great diversity surrounding him, but he believed that

an even greater unity supported the diversity and his own work was an expression        9c

of that unity.

## EXERCISE 10-1    Needed words: Guided practice

Add any words needed for grammatical or logical completeness in the following paragraphs. The numbers in the margin refer to appropriate rules in section 10 of *Rules for Writers*, Sixth Edition. The first revision has been done for you, and a suggested revision of this exercise appears in the back of the book.

Mary Wollstonecraft, an eighteenth-century writer, may have been England's first feminist. Her entire life reflected her belief in equal rights for women in all areas of their lives: personal, intellectual, and professional.

From childhood, she never had and never would accept the idea that men were superior to women. As a young girl, she knew that her drinking and gambling father deserved less respect than her long-suffering mother. As an adult, she demanded that society give her the same freedom it gave to men.

*10a*

Wollstonecraft also demanded men pay attention to her ideas. She did not argue about an idea. Instead, she gave an example of what she objected to and invited her readers to think about it from various points of view. Working this way, she made few enemies among intellectuals. Indeed, she was attracted and respected by some of the leading intellectuals of her day. Among them she was as well known on one side of the Atlantic as on the other. Tom Paine, the American orator and writer, probably knew her better than Samuel Johnson, the English writer.

*10b*

*10a*

*10c*

Professionally, she was a governess, teacher, and writer. When her father's drinking destroyed the family, she and her sisters started a girls' school. Eventually, financial problems forced the school to close, but not before Mary had acquired enough firsthand experience to write *Thoughts on the Education of Daughters* (1786). As competent or more competent than other writers of the day, she was a more persuasive advocate for women than most of them.

*10c*

Modern feminists may find it ironic that current encyclopedia entries for "Wollstonecraft" refer researchers to "Godwin," her married name—where they will find an entry for her longer than her famous husband, William Godwin.

*10c*

**EXERCISE 10-2**    **Needed words**    To read about this topic, see section 10 in *Rules for Writers*, Sixth Edition.

Circle the letter of the clearer sentence in each pair. Example:

    a. Mary Wollstonecraft felt a woman did not have to marry a man in order to live with him.

    (b.) Mary Wollstonecraft felt that a woman did not have to marry a man in order to live with him.

1a.  She never married, or wanted to, her first suitor.

  b.  She never married, or wanted to marry, her first suitor.

2a.  With Gilbert Imlay, she discovered that travel could teach her much about the business world.

  b.  With Gilbert Imlay, she discovered travel could teach her much about the business world.

3a.  She had a more intellectual relationship with William Godwin than Gilbert Imlay.

  b.  She had a more intellectual relationship with William Godwin than with Gilbert Imlay.

4a.  In one way she may have been as conservative as, if not more conservative than, other women of her day.

  b.  In one way she may have been as conservative, if not more conservative, than other women of her day.

5a.  Marrying Godwin when she became pregnant may have shown that she believed in and acted by society's rules for pregnant women.

  b.  Marrying Godwin when she became pregnant may have shown that she believed and acted by society's rules for pregnant women.

## EXERCISE 10-3    Needed words    To read about this topic, see section 10 in *Rules for Writers*, Sixth Edition.

Missing words make some of the following sentences ambiguous. Add the needed words so that only one meaning is possible. If a sentence is clear as written, mark it "OK." Example:

*did.*

**Mary Wollstonecraft approved of the French Revolution more than Edmund Burke/**
                                                                   ^

1. Wollstonecraft blamed women's problems on the structure of society more than the men of her time.

2. Her ideas about women frightened other people less than her husband.

3. One of her daughters, Mary Shelley, who wrote *Frankenstein*, became as famous as Wollstonecraft herself.

4. The readers Mary Shelley attracted were different from those who enjoyed her mother's work.

5. Modern readers know Mary Shelley better than Mary Wollstonecraft.

## EXERCISE 10-4    Needed words: Guided review

Add any words needed for grammatical or logical completeness in the following paragraphs. The numbers in the margin refer to appropriate rules in section 10 of *Rules for Writers*, Sixth Edition. The first revision has been done for you.

*that*
Most people in her era found ∧ Mary Wollstonecraft used very persuasive tech-                    10b

niques. She did not argue and never had by directly attacking those who disagreed                    10a

with her.

More astute than other women of her day, she used anecdotal "observations."

She knew disarming stories and anecdotes would make her point best. Since she did                    10b

not argue, her listeners never felt they had to defend their own positions and were

able to listen to her stories with reasonably open minds. The stories, which often

made clever use of allegory and metaphor, came from her own experience and ob-

servation. Preferring examples from dressmaking to other occupations, she chose                    10c

stories that illustrated her points and let the anecdotes speak for themselves. Her

technique was as convincing, or more convincing than, outright argument.                    10c

Mary Wollstonecraft's sense of timing was also good. In 1790, she wrote a pam-

phlet entitled *A Vindication of the Rights of Men.* Part of her reason for writing it was

to respond to the excitement caused by the French Revolution (1789–1799). People

liked her pamphlet very much. While enthusiasm was still high, she produced *A

Vindication of the Rights of Women* in 1792. It, too, was well received.

No doubt part of Mary Wollstonecraft's unusually effective writing came from

the fact that she not only believed in but also lived the ideas she wrote about.                    10a

## EXERCISE 11-1    Mixed constructions: Guided practice

Edit the following paragraphs to eliminate problems with mixed constructions. The numbers in the margin refer to appropriate rules in section 11 of *Rules for Writers*, Sixth Edition. The first revision has been done for you, and a suggested revision of this exercise appears in the back of the book.

Sometimes it's hard to separate fact from fiction, to know what is history and what is folklore. Casey Jones, John Henry, Johnny Appleseed, Uncle Sam, Santa Claus—which of these ~~names~~ were real men? Although we've been told stories about      *11b*
them all of our lives, but are those stories true?      *11a*

There really was a railroad engineer people called "Casey" Jones; the reason he got that nickname was because of his birthplace, Cayce, Kentucky. There really was      *11c*
a "Cannonball" too; it was the Illinois-Central's fast mail train. And there really was a train wreck: Engine Number 382 rammed into some freight cars. The accident was not Casey's fault, and Casey died trying to save his passengers. When workers found his body in the wreckage, his hand was still on the air-brake lever. (The use of air      *11b*
brakes had recently been installed on trains to increase their braking power.)

John Henry was an African American railroad worker of great strength. In legend and song, he died after a timed contest against a steam drill. By using a hammer in each hand made him win the contest. John Henry drilled two holes seven feet      *11a*
deep; the steam drill bored only one nine-foot hole. The real John Henry died on the job too, crushed by rocks that fell from the ceiling of a railroad tunnel.

John Chapman, better known as Johnny Appleseed, was a wealthy and well-liked nurseryman who kept moving his place of business west as the frontier moved west. His boyhood friend Sam Wilson supplied meat to the US troops during the War of 1812. A worker told a government inspector that the "US" stamped on the meat stood for "Uncle Sam." Although it was a joke, but it caught on, and Congress made      *11a*
the "Uncle Sam" identification official in the 1960s.

That leaves Santa Claus. As far as historians know now, Santa was not real. But legends say that there was once a man who . . .

---

Correct the mixed constructions in the following sentences. Example:

> What European first set eyes on America? If you say Amerigo Vespucci, from whom the name "America" is said to derive, ~~so~~ you'll be only half right.

1. Although Vespucci claimed to have found a new continent, but there is no evidence that he ever got to any land in the Western Hemisphere.

2. Columbus may have seen parts of the Americas first, but when a German mapmaker believed Vespucci's claim and put Vespucci's name on the map explains why the lands became known as America.

3. If Vespucci wasn't the first European to find land across the Atlantic, so who was?

4. For most British historians who have worked on the question say John Cabot got there first.

5. Early mariners, a very dangerous occupation, often sailed under several names.

6. "John Cabot" was the name for Italian mariner Giovanni Caboto used when he worked for the English.

7. Some people say that Leif Eriksson saw the coast of North America first; their reason is because he established a small community on Newfoundland about AD 1000.

8. Even though Eriksson's community was established five hundred years before the time of Vespucci, Columbus, and Cabot, but the Norse sagas claim that Bjarni Herjulfsson sighted North America before Eriksson did.

9. The growth in the number of theories increases as new evidence is found.

10. So who was the first European on American shores? As these bits of history indicate that no one can really answer that question.

**EXERCISE 11-3    Mixed constructions**    To read about this topic, see section 11 in *Rules for Writers*, Sixth Edition.

Read through each sentence just once. If it sounds correct to you, put "OK" after it. If it sounds like a mixed construction, put "MC" after it. Then go back and check; only four of the sentences should have "OK" after them. Fix the others. Example:

Do you believe that ~~because of~~ Paul Revere's late-night horseback ride alerted Minutemen from Boston to Lexington to Concord that the British were coming? ___*MC*___

1. In college, most American students discover that their knowledge of history is a mixture of fact and fiction. _____

2. For example, most students believe that Paul Revere rode alone, alerting citizens from Boston to Concord that the British were coming. In fact, Revere did not ride alone, and he never made it to Concord. _____

3. Since he was able to borrow a horse permitted Revere to get as far as Lexington. _____

4. By adding two other riders, William Dawes and Samuel Prescott, made it possible to get the warning to Concord. _____

5. The vigilance of a group of British soldiers on patrol overtook all three men, captured Revere, and found out who he was. _____

6. The reason Minutemen reported promptly for duty was because they were warned by relays of riders who had been alerted by prearranged signals. _____

7. If Henry Wadsworth Longfellow had not written a poem about the ride forty-five years after Revere's death, so Revere might never have become famous. _____

8. Before that poem appeared, Paul Revere's name was not on any list of important people in America. _____

9. The increase in the number of times his name appeared on such lists after the poem was published was enough to make him famous. _____

10. Is fiction more powerful than fact? Is all our knowledge such a mixture of fact and fiction? _____

## EXERCISE 11-4    Mixed constructions: Guided review

Edit the following paragraphs to eliminate problems with mixed constructions. The numbers in the margin refer to appropriate rules in section 11 of *Rules for Writers,* Sixth Edition. The first revision has been done for you.

What did Paul Revere do when he wasn't working for the Revolution? Quite apart from his famous ride, Paul Revere made other significant contributions to American life and culture.

The basic reason for all these contributions was ~~because~~ *that* Paul Revere was an    11c
enterprising entrepreneur. He originally followed his father into silversmithing. Soon after the war started, he began making gunpowder. He designed and printed paper money and made the state seal that Massachusetts still uses. By carving false teeth    11a
from rhinoceros tusks was one of his efforts to make money; publishing hymnbooks was another. He engraved copper plates for printing. He ran a hardware store and erected barns for local farmers.

Until Revere built the first rolling mill for copper in the United States, so all    11a
rolled copper had to be imported. He set up the equipment to cast bronze and made cannon for the army, copper fittings for the USS *Constitution* (Old Ironsides), and bells for churches. Seventy-five of his bells still ring from New England church steeples.

As a silversmith, a very creative field, Revere displayed great skill. His silver    11b
pieces were so beautifully crafted that two hundred years later one of his punch bowls brought an offer of a hundred thousand dollars. One reason that antique lovers today search for silver objects marked "Revere" is because Revere's work is so    11c
graceful. Modern artisans still try to duplicate his decorated grooves and flowing lines. And shoppers admire certain smoothly curved bowls are known as Revere    11a
bowls whether they are made of silver or of some other metal.

Whether or not he rode all the way to Concord, Paul Revere made an indelible impression on American life and culture.

## EXERCISE 12-1    Misplaced and dangling modifiers: Guided practice

Edit the following paragraphs to eliminate misplaced and dangling modifiers. The numbers in the margin refer to appropriate rules in section 12 of *Rules for Writers*, Sixth Edition. The first revision has been done for you, and a suggested revision of this exercise appears in the back of the book.

*people usually think first of*

Hearing the name Karl Marx, Russia, ~~is usually the first thought that comes to~~      *12e*

~~mind~~. Marx never lived in Russia at all. Actually, he almost spent all of his adult life      *12a*

in England. He was a political exile for the last half of his life.

Marx lived first in Germany. Born of Jewish parents, his university studies      *12e*

were completed with a PhD at the University of Jena. His favorite professor tried to

get Marx an appointment to teach at the university. When that professor was fired,

Marx gave up hope of teaching at Jena or any other German university. Marx, be-      *12c*

cause he was denied a university position, had to earn his living as a journalist. He

worked briefly as a newspaper editor in Germany.

Next came France, Belgium, and a return to Germany. First Marx and his new

bride moved to Paris, where Marx worked for a radical journal and became friendly

with Friedrich Engels. When the journal ceased publication, Marx moved to

Brussels, Belgium, and then back to Cologne, Germany. He did not hold a regular      *12d*

job, so he tried desperately to at least earn enough money to feed his family.

Marx decided after living in Paris and Brussels he would settle in London. He      *12b*

and his family lived in abject poverty while Marx earned what little income he could

by writing for an American newspaper, the *New York Tribune*.

**EXERCISE 12-2**    **Misplaced modifiers**    To read about this topic, see section 12 in *Rules for Writers*, Sixth Edition.

---

Circle the letter of the more effective sentence in each pair. Example:

  a. Marx almost spent all his time writing, using every waking moment to get his ideas down on paper.

  (b.) Marx spent almost all his time writing, using every waking moment to get his ideas down on paper.

1a. Between 1852 and 1862, Marx just wrote more than three hundred articles for the *New York Tribune.*

  b. Between 1852 and 1862, Marx wrote more than three hundred articles just for the *New York Tribune.*

2a. During his lifetime, Marx did not receive much attention. But people all over the world paid attention to what he had written after his death.

  b. During his lifetime, Marx did not receive much attention. But after his death, people all over the world paid attention to what he had written.

3a. He wanted only one thing for himself: recognition of the importance of his ideas.

  b. He only wanted one thing for himself: recognition of the importance of his ideas.

4a. Capitalist scholars tend to usually say that Marx's work is "illogical" and "uninformed."

  b. Capitalist scholars usually tend to say that Marx's work is "illogical" and "uninformed."

5a. However, most capitalists agree that as a student of social organization he was brilliant.

  b. However, most capitalists agree that he, as a student of social organization, was brilliant.

## EXERCISE 12-3    Misplaced and dangling modifiers    To read about this topic, see section 12 in *Rules for Writers,* Sixth Edition.

Circle the letter of the more effective sentence in each pair. Be prepared to explain your choice. Example:

   a. Deciding that there were two classes of people in the world, they were named the "bourgeoisie" and the "proletariat."

   (b.) Deciding that there were two classes of people in the world, Marx named them the "bourgeoisie" and the "proletariat."

1a. Convinced that one major difference divided the people of the world into two groups, ownership of property was declared the basis for this division.

   b. Convinced that one major difference divided the people of the world into two groups, Marx declared that ownership of property was the basis for this division.

2a. Marx defined anyone who owned property as bourgeois.

   b. Owning property of any kind, the property defined its owner as bourgeois.

3a. Marx defined the proletariat as those who owned no property but labored to always produce wealth for the bourgeoisie.

   b. Marx defined the proletariat as those who owned no property but always labored to produce wealth for the bourgeoisie.

4a. After finishing his study of economic history, Marx concluded that history is progressive and maybe even inevitable.

   b. Marx, after finishing his study of economic history, concluded that history is progressive and maybe even inevitable.

5a. Denying God any role in human affairs, economic history was seen as a natural evolution in the world.

   b. Denying God any role in human affairs, Marx saw economic history as a natural evolution in the world.

## EXERCISE 12-4   Misplaced and dangling modifiers: Guided review

Edit the following paragraphs to eliminate misplaced and dangling modifiers. The numbers in the margin refer to appropriate rules in section 12 of *Rules for Writers*, Sixth Edition. The first revision has been done for you.

Marx wrote *The Communist Manifesto,* his most famous work, in collaboration with Friedrich Engels just before the German revolution of 1848. The book has three sections with distinct characteristics.

In the first part, Marx tries to ~~accurately~~ *accurately* define terms and to state his basic as-     12d
sumptions. He traces the class systems of earlier times and concludes that there are only two classes in his day, the bourgeoisie and the proletariat. The bourgeoisie are the property-owning capitalists; the proletariat are the working class. Marx asserts that as the bourgeoisie increase their economic power, they work toward their own eventual downfall.

Set up in question-and-answer format, Marx made the second section of his     12e
*Communist Manifesto* resemble a debate with a bourgeois sympathizer. Of course, Marx only sees one side of the debate as being correct. After "defeating" his oppo-     12a
nent on major questions, Marx presents his own ten-point program in clear, easy-to-understand, persuasive language.

Marx, after developing the second part in detail, moves on to the final section     12c
of the *Manifesto.* He shows how **Communists** and other reform groups work toward the same goals. Reminding workers that **they "have nothing to lose** but their chains,"     12d
Marx calls on them to zealously and actively **work together.** Marx utters the slogan     12b
that can still be heard today in ringing tones: "Workers of the world, unite!"

## EXERCISE 13-1    Distracting shifts: Guided practice

Edit the following paragraphs to eliminate distracting shifts. The numbers in the margin refer to appropriate rules in section 13 of *Rules for Writers,* Sixth Edition. The first revision has been done for you, and a suggested revision of this exercise appears in the back of the book.

Do you know how slavery began in America or how ~~did it end?~~ *it ended?* When the        13d
*Mayflower* landed in September 1620, slaves were already in America. A Dutch ship
had unloaded and sold twenty Africans in Jamestown, Virginia, the year before.

Actually, slavery in America began long before that. Many early explorers
brought slaves with them to the new land, and some historians claim that one of the
men in Christopher Columbus's crew was a slave. From the 1500s to the 1800s,
slave ships brought ten million African slaves across the ocean.

Most of the slaves stayed in Latin America and the West Indies, but the southern part of the United States receives about 6 percent of them. Few northerners        13b
owned slaves, and opposition to slavery was evident by the time of the American
Revolution. Rhode Island prohibited the importation of slaves even before the
Revolutionary War. After the war, six northern states abolished slavery at once.
Others passed laws to phase out slavery, and even Virginia enacted legislation encouraging you to emancipate your slaves.        13a

But it took a war, a tricky political situation, and a very clever former slave to
free all slaves. History gives Lincoln the credit for liberating the slaves during the
Civil War, and he deserves some credit, but emancipation was not his idea.
Originally, no one in government seriously considered emancipation because they        13a
were so focused on winning the war to save the Union. Then an important black man        13b
talks to Lincoln and gives him the idea and the reason. This man said that freeing        13d
slaves would be good for the war effort and would Lincoln agree to do it? Who was
this man? He was Frederick Douglass, fugitive slave and newspaper editor.

## EXERCISE 13-2   Distracting shifts     To read about this topic, see section 13 in
*Rules for Writers*, Sixth Edition.

A.  Edit the following sentences to eliminate distracting pronoun shifts. If a sentence is correct, mark it "OK." Example:

Frederick Douglass was born a slave, but he was lucky because his owner's wife did not know that
*her*
it was against the law for ~~you~~ to teach a slave to read and write.
                            ^

 1.  A slave who learned to read and write gained self-confidence, so they were harder to over-see than illiterate slaves.

 2.  When he had learned enough to study on his own, the slave Frederick Douglass did so; he used what he had learned to escape from his owner.

 3.  The master had told his slaves that all escape routes were blocked and that you would have no chance whatever at success.

 4.  Douglass used a simple but dangerous method of escape; he sailed from Baltimore to New York as a working sailor.

 5.  A listener could not learn anything about escape routes from Douglass's stories because Douglass told them nothing that would endanger other fugitives.

B.  Edit the following sentences to eliminate distracting shifts in verb tense. If a sentence is correct, mark it "OK." Example:

                                                          *describes*
Douglass's narrative tells about his own life as a child and ~~described~~ his torturous beatings by a
                                                              ^
professional "slave breaker."

 6.  Douglass had few ties to his mother and never meets his father.

 7.  Even when Douglass worked "out" for his master, his master got his wages.

 8.  His master sometimes allowed him to keep 1 percent (six cents out of six dollars); the master thought the money would encourage Douglass to work harder.

 9.  Douglass escapes by pretending to be someone else; he borrowed the identification papers of a freed black sailor.

10.  Frederick Douglass used several different names as he escaped slavery; an abolitionist friend suggests "Douglass" to him and Frederick uses it from that time on.

**EXERCISE 13-3    Distracting shifts**    To read about this topic, see section 13 in *Rules for Writers*, Sixth Edition.

---

Edit the following sentences to eliminate shifts between direct and indirect quotation or question. Example:

*whether he*
When Frederick was told to choose a new name, he asked could ~~he~~ keep "Frederick" and take a new
^
last name.

1.  When a friend suggested "Douglass" as a last name, Frederick asked whether it was a satisfactory name and did it fit well with "Frederick"?

2.  People frequently asked Douglass how did he feel when he found himself in a free state.

3.  Lonely and frightened at the time, he said, "I can trust no man" and that he saw every white man as an enemy, every black man as a cause for distrust.

4.  Douglass was befriended by David Ruggles, an abolitionist who asked him what did he plan to do.

5.  Douglass married Anna and told her that they would move to New Bedford and don't worry because he would surely get a job there.

## EXERCISE 13-4    Distracting shifts: Guided review

Edit the following paragraphs to eliminate any distracting shifts. The numbers in the margin refer to appropriate rules in section 13 of *Rules for Writers*, Sixth Edition. The first revision has been done for you.

Frederick Douglass, who was born a slave and became a much sought-after lecturer and writer, was a man of strong will and convictions.

Douglass never hesitated to defend the choices he ~~makes~~ *made* for himself and his                13b
family. On trains he sat in cars reserved for "whites only" until security officers
dragged him away. He walked out of a church when it was realized that none of his                13c
people could participate in the service until the white people were finished.

Wherever he lived, Douglass fought slavery. When he published his autobiography, *Narrative of the Life of Frederick Douglass,* in 1845, he was still a fugitive
slave. He and his wife moved to England the same year because he feared that his
book would reveal his identity as a fugitive slave. Also, some of his other writings
had aroused so much animosity that he fears for his life. From England, he wrote                13b
letters and worked to gain support for freeing the slaves. After friends in England
raised enough money to buy his freedom for him, he was even more determined to
help others gain their freedom. (Slaves used to say that a free black was never there
when you needed help, but no one could ever say that about Frederick Douglass.)                13a

Douglass was outspoken in his support for the causes he believed in. When the
Civil War broke out, Douglass comes back to the United States to help recruit                13b
African Americans to fight. "This war is for you and your children," he told them.
Douglass also supported woman suffrage, and he defended the right of members of
different races to marry if they wished. When Douglass married his second wife, a
white woman, critics complained. He answered them by saying, "My first wife was
the color of my mother" and that the second was the color of his father, so he was                13d
not playing favorites.

## EXERCISE 14-1    Emphasis: Guided practice

Edit the following paragraph to put major ideas in independent clauses and minor ideas in subordinate clauses or phrases. The numbers in the margin refer to appropriate rules in section 14 of *Rules for Writers,* Sixth Edition. The first revision has been done for you, and a suggested revision of this exercise appears in the back of the book.

No one who knew Albert Einstein as a young child would ever have believed that he might one day be called the smartest man in the world. None of his teachers could have predicted success for him. ~~Albert was a~~ *A shy,* slow learner, ~~He was shy. He~~ *Albert* always    14b

got into trouble in class. He consistently failed some subjects. They were the subjects he did not like. His family could not have predicted his success either. Albert    14b

could not even get to meals on time. Night after night his parents had to postpone dinner until servants searched the house and grounds and found the boy, at which    14e

time he would be full of apologies but have no explanation to offer for his lateness except that he was "thinking." Once his angry father dangled his big gold watch at    14b

Albert. He told Albert to figure out how late he was. Albert, who was fascinated by    14d

the tiny magnetic compass hanging from the watch chain, could not tell time. The boy asked so many questions about the compass that he did not eat much dinner anyway. Albert begged his father to lend him the compass to sleep with, and his fa-    14c

ther let him borrow it. Years later Einstein wondered whether that little compass had been the beginning of his interest in science.

**EXERCISE 14-2**     **Emphasis**     To read about this topic, see section 14 in *Rules for Writers*, Sixth Edition.

Combine or restructure the following sentences so that the independent clause expresses the idea in brackets and everything else is subordinated. Example:

*who owned an electrochemical factory,*
Albert Einstein's father, Hermann Einstein, had some interest in science. ~~He owned an electro-~~
∧
~~chemical factory.~~ [*Emphasize his father's interest in science.*]

1. Hermann Einstein moved his electrochemical business to Munich; the move made it possible for his son to have the best schooling available. [*Emphasize the fact that Hermann moved his business.*]

2. Albert Einstein's Uncle Jake explained math to the boy and made algebra problems into games. [*Emphasize Uncle Jake's making games out of the problems.*]

3. Albert's mother was impressed by her son's persistent questions and secretly hoped that Albert would one day be a professor. [*Emphasize the mother's hope.*]

4. One of Albert's friends was a medical student at the University of Munich. This friend supplied Albert with well-written modern books on natural science. [*Emphasize that the friend supplied Einstein with books.*]

5. Hermann Einstein kept his business in Munich for several years, and afterward he decided to go to Italy and work with relatives. [*Emphasize the decision to go to Italy and work with relatives.*]

**EXERCISE 14-3**     **Emphasis**     To read about this topic, see section 14 in *Rules for Writers*, Sixth Edition.

---

Combine or restructure the following sentences so that the independent clause expresses the idea mentioned in brackets. Example:

> *When*
> Hermann Einstein moved his family to Italy, ~~but~~ he left Albert in Munich to finish school.
> ^
> [*Emphasize his leaving Albert in Munich to finish school.*]

1. Albert was miserably lonely without his family, and he had always depended on them for his social life. [*Emphasize Albert's loneliness without his family.*]

2. He did not get along with the other students. He did not get along with his teachers either. [*Emphasize both ideas equally.*]

3. He had never gotten along well with other students, and they envied his superior work in math and physics. [*Emphasize his not getting along with other students.*]

4. In mathematics he was smarter than his teachers, so his teachers resented him too. [*Emphasize his teachers' resentment of him.*]

5. He was desperate to be with his family in sunny Italy, so he faked a nervous breakdown. [*Emphasize his faking a nervous breakdown.*]

6. Albert convinced a medical doctor to sign a formal request for a six-month vacation, and then he found out that the school had expelled him. [*Emphasize his discovery that the school had expelled him.*]

7. His months in Italy were a welcome change, and they gave him time to enjoy life again and to plan for his future. [*Emphasize that the months in Italy were welcome.*]

8. Albert spent months thinking about his future while he enjoyed Italy's scenery, art, and music, and then he finally decided that he wanted to be a theoretical physicist. [*Emphasize his decision to become a theoretical physicist.*]

9. He knew his father's business was not doing well, but he asked his father for enough money to take the entrance exams at the Swiss Federal Polytechnic School. [*Emphasize his request to his father.*]

10. His father wanted him to succeed, so he found the money somehow. [*Emphasize his father's finding the money.*]

## EXERCISE 14-4    Emphasis: Guided review

Edit the following paragraph to put major ideas in independent clauses and minor ideas in subordinate clauses or phrases. The numbers in the margin refer to appropriate rules in section 14 of *Rules for Writers,* Sixth Edition. The first revision has been done for you.

    Teachers are not always right about their pupils. Certainly Albert Einstein's teachers, ~~misjudged~~ *misjudging* his ability in math, ~~and they~~ failed to spot the most brilliant stu-      *14c*

dent they had ever had. Giuseppe Verdi's teachers made similar errors in judging

their pupil's musical ability. Verdi was Italian. He lived in the nineteenth century.      *14b*

He wanted to be a composer. He applied to the Conservatory of Music in Milan, and      *14c*

he was rejected because he "showed no aptitude for music." Today his works are

performed more than those of any other opera composer. Scientists have also been

underestimated. Everyone has heard of Charles Darwin, the British scientist. This      *14d*

man, who also had trouble in school, first proposed the theory of evolution. He did

so poorly at his school, which was the University of Edinburgh, that his teachers      *14e*

considered him hopeless, as a result of which they dismissed him. The first

American physicist to win the Nobel Prize for physics was also misjudged by his

teachers. Albert Abraham Michelson was a student at Annapolis. He was in the      *14b*

naval academy there. One of his teachers told him to pay less attention to science

and concentrate on naval gunnery. Luckily, Einstein, Verdi, Darwin, and Michelson

refused to accept their teachers' evaluations of them.

## EXERCISE 15-1    Variety: Guided practice

The following paragraphs are grammatically correct but dull. Revise them to add variety. You may need to combine some sentences. The numbers in the margin refer to appropriate revision strategies in section 15 of *Rules for Writers,* Sixth Edition. The first revision has been done for you, and a suggested revision of this exercise appears in the back of the book.

Everyone has heard of Martin Luther King Jr. ~~He studied~~ *After studying* for the ministry at     15a, 15b
Boston University and ~~earned~~ *earning* a doctorate in theology, ~~and then~~ he went home to the     *(See also 14c.)*
South to work as a minister. He started working in civil rights and became the most
influential leader of that cause in America. When he died, the victim of an assassin's
bullet, his name was almost synonymous with "civil rights." Historians and biographers have recorded his leadership in the fight to gain basic civil rights for all
Americans. Many people who know of his civil rights work, however, are not aware
of his skill as a writer. King produced other important writing in addition to his care-     15a
fully crafted and emotional speeches.

King's "Letter from Birmingham Jail" is among his most famous writings. He     15c
wrote it to answer a statement published by eight Alabama ministers that King's     15a, 15b
*(See also 14c.)*
work was "unwise and untimely," and the letter shows King to be a man who had
great patience with his critics. King is eager to get these ministers to accept his point     15b
*(See also 14c.)*
of view, so he reminds them that they are ministers. Their goodwill, he says, should
help them see that his views hold value. He does not attack them personally. He an-     15b
*(See also 14b.)*
alyzes their arguments. Then he presents his own views. Does he use many of the
emotional appeals for which he is justly famous? No, in this letter King depends on
logic and reasoning as the tools to win his argument.

**EXERCISE 15-2**    **Variety**    To read about this topic, see section 15 in *Rules for Writers*, Sixth Edition.

Edit each of the following sentences in at least two ways, to provide varied openings and varied sentence structures. You may need to change other parts of the sentence as well. Example:

                                    *In*                    *Martin Luther King Jr.*
    a. ~~Martin Luther King Jr. was in~~ jail awaiting a hearing/, ~~he~~ read a newspaper article attacking his
                        ^                                    ^
       work.
       *When*
    b. Martin Luther King Jr. was in jail awaiting a hearing/, he read a newspaper article attacking his
       ^                                                      ^
       work.

1a. King didn't have much to write on in the jail, so he started writing on the margins of the

    newspaper in which the article appeared.

 b. King didn't have much to write on in the jail, so he started writing on the margins of the

    newspaper in which the article appeared.

2a. A black trusty, wanting to help King, was able to get some scraps of paper for him after a

    while.

 b. A black trusty, wanting to help King, was able to get some scraps of paper for him after a

    while.

3a. His attorneys were later allowed to give him a pad of paper. King, fired up by the newspa-

    per article, quickly filled the pad.

 b. His attorneys were later allowed to give him a pad of paper. King, fired up by the newspa-

    per article, quickly filled the pad.

4a. King chose to write his response to the newspaper article in letter form, so he seemed like

    the biblical Paul to some people.

 b. King chose to write his response to the newspaper article in letter form, so he seemed like

    the biblical Paul to some people.

5a. How were King and Paul alike? Paul, a preacher of the Christian faith like King, wrote some

    of his famous letters from a prison cell.

 b. How were King and Paul alike? Paul, a preacher of the Christian faith like King, wrote some

    of his famous letters from a prison cell.

## EXERCISE 15-3    Variety: Guided review

The following paragraph is grammatically correct but dull. Revise it to add variety. You may need to combine some sentences. The numbers in the margin refer to appropriate revision strategies in section 15 of *Rules for Writers*, Sixth Edition. The first revision has been done for you.

Martin Luther King's famous "Letter from Birmingham Jail" has a clearly thought-out structure. ~~King begins~~ *Beginning* with the statement that any nonviolent campaign has to go through four distinct stages/ ~~He says these stages are~~ fact finding,      15b or 15a
negotiation, self-purification, and direct action/ ~~He~~ *King* says that he and his fellow campaigners have gone through all these steps in Birmingham. King tries to reach his readers after that beginning by asking them how to answer his children's questions      15b
about why they cannot go to the amusement park advertised on TV. The letter discusses the difference between just and unjust laws, and it emphasizes the need for      15b or 15a
(See also 14c.)
nonviolent direct action to dramatize the unjust ones. Next King mentions the "white moderates." He expresses his disappointment with white religious leaders and white churches who have failed to join the civil rights movement, but he praises the few who have helped. He describes the mistreatment he and his friends have suffered at      15b or 15a
(See also 14c.)
the hands of the local police, and he gives thanks for the courage of the people involved in sit-ins and bus strikes. King writes finally of his faith that the movement      15a
will survive and prosper and that racial prejudice will soon pass away.

## REVIEW OF 8–15:  Clarity (effective sentences)

Edit the following paragraphs for sentence problems. Section numbers in the margin refer to suggested revision strategies in *Rules for Writers*, Sixth Edition. The first revision has been done for you.

One of the men who greatly influenced Martin Luther King Jr. was Mahatma
Gandhi, ~~and he~~ *who* introduced nonviolent protest techniques in Africa and India.    14c
Gandhi is called the father of his country, and he helped India gain its freedom from    14c
England. Gandhi's nonviolent method was based on three principles: courage, being
truthful, and you had to have endurance. By using nonviolent techniques is how    9a, 11a
Gandhi helped Indians in Africa and India.

After studying law in London, he attempts to practice law in India but is not    13b
very successful. When he went to South Africa to do legal work in 1893, he was
abused because he was an Indian who also claimed the rights of a British subject.
Although he had planned to stay in Africa one year, he remained for twenty-one
years. Fighting injustice in South Africa, the principle of *satyagraha* (nonviolent    12e
protest) was developed by Gandhi during those years.    8a

After working in South Africa, Gandhi returned to India to lead the Indian
movement for independence. While in India, he led hundreds of his followers on a
march to the sea. There they made salt from seawater to protest a law. That law re-    14b
quired them to buy all their salt from the government. He also began programs of
hand weaving and spinning among the poor that exist to this day.    12b

Although Gandhi believed and lived by the nonviolent principle of *satyagraha,*    10a
he died a violent death. In 1948 he was assassinated by a high-caste Hindu fanatic.
This man feared Gandhi's tolerance for all creeds and religions. Nevertheless,    14b
Gandhi's nonviolent methods have survived to this day. When Martin Luther King
Jr. began his civil rights work in the United States, many people compared him to
Gandhi, saying that his principles were essentially the same as Gandhi.    10c

## EXERCISE 16-1    Wordy sentences: Guided practice

Edit the following paragraph to make any wordy sentences as short as possible without changing their meaning. The numbers in the margin refer to appropriate revision strategies in section 16 of *Rules for Writers*, Sixth Edition. The first two revisions have been done for you, and a suggested revision of this exercise appears in the back of the book.

Adam Smith, the founder of modern economics, proposed a theory in the eighteenth century that has made him controversial ever since. This ~~British~~ economist, *16a*

~~who was~~ born in Scotland and educated in England, wrote the first complete study *16e*

of political economy. *The Wealth of Nations* was published in the same year that

Americans declared their independence from England—that was in 1776. Smith's *16e*

book pointed out and directed attention to the interdependence of freedom and or- *16a*

der, economic processes, and free-trade laws. Although Smith's thinking did not

really affect economic policies significantly during his lifetime, its influence in the

next century was considerable. Among economists, "the invisible hand" and "laissez-

faire" are synonymous with Smith's name. History has only made Smith's ideas

more controversial. Say "Adam Smith" to conservative businesspeople, and those *16b*

same people will smile and make a response with words like "He was a good *16d*

man—really understood how business works!" Say "Adam Smith" to liberal reform-

ers, and they will grimace and mutter something along the lines of "He was an evil *16c*

man—really sold the average citizen down the river." Both of these reactions are ex-

treme, but such responses indicate that the controversy aroused by Smith's ideas is

still alive.

**EXERCISE 16-2** **Wordy sentences** To read about this topic, see section 16 in *Rules for Writers*, Sixth Edition.

Tighten the following sentences by eliminating redundancies, unnecessary repetition, and empty phrases. The number in parentheses at the end of each sentence is a suggested maximum number of words for your revision. Example:

                                                      to
~~It is a fact that~~ Adam Smith wanted to find a theory ~~that would~~ explain how the economic world
                                                      ^
functions. (14)

1.  It seems that after many years of study and then years of writing, he published a book that was called *The Wealth of Nations.* (14)

2.  This lengthy, protracted book had in the neighborhood of a thousand pages, and those pages included a sixty-three-page index. (12)

3.  The full and complete title of his book indicates the comprehensive, all-inclusive scope of the book: *An Inquiry into the Nature and Causes of the Wealth of Nations.* (19. Do not shorten the twelve-word title.)

4.  Smith believed that there are certain basic, essential economic laws in existence and that these laws work to the benefit of everyone if people "let the market alone." (17)

5.  He believed that something along the lines of an "invisible hand" guides economics. (10)

## EXERCISE 16-3    Wordy sentences    To read about this topic, see section 16 in
*Rules for Writers,* Sixth Edition.

Tighten the following sentences without changing their meaning. The number in parentheses at the end of each sentence is a suggested maximum number of words for your revision. Example:

> Adam Smith saw the market as ~~something that is~~ "self-regulating" ~~as long as~~ *if* everyone leaves it alone. (12)

1.  Adam Smith said that there are two laws that govern the field of economics. (8)

2.  The first basic, important, essential law that governs the field of economics is self-interest. (5, but can you do it in 3?)

3.  The one who is employed wants a higher wage; the one who employs the worker wants a higher profit. (12)

4.  The second law, which is the law of competition, works only if there is no manipulation of the market by anyone. (12)

5.  Because people will buy the gloves that cost the least, a manufacturer of gloves cannot raise prices for gloves too much without bringing about the result that people who buy gloves go to competitors who sell gloves for a lower price. (25)

6.  The term that has been given to Smith's "let the market alone" policy by economists is "laissez-faire." (9)

7.  Adam Smith urged governments to practice the policy of laissez-faire with the resulting effect that it would allow "the invisible hand" to regulate the marketplace. (16)

8.  Smith assumed that there was a "law of accumulation" that works by requiring industrialists to add buildings and machinery, to hire more workers, and to produce more goods. (23)

9.  There was another law that he called the "law of population" that supplies the workers that are necessary. (10)

10. In the long run, said Smith, those who do the work will be paid, the industrialists who employ those who do the work will make a fair profit, and the landlords who rent space to the industrialists will have many tenants. (21)

## EXERCISE 16-4    Wordy sentences: Guided review

Edit the following paragraph to make any wordy sentences as short as possible without changing their meaning. The numbers in the margin refer to appropriate revision strategies in section 16 of *Rules for Writers*, Sixth Edition. The first wordy sentence has been revised for you.

Adam Smith was convinced ~~in his mind~~ that if people would "let the market          *16a*

alone," all would be well. The true facts about how the market operated during the          *16a*

next century would have distressed him. The industrialists chose Smith as the pa-

tron saint for industrialists. Working to make sure that the government "let the mar-          *16b*

ket alone," they opposed even laws that forbade shackling children to the machines

that were operated by them. By means of agreements that were secret, they agreed          *16d, 16e*

to charge identical prices. Similarly, workers agreed to demand the same wages from

every employer. Neither employers nor employees followed Adam Smith's injunction

to let the market alone. It seems quite obvious that there can be no doubt that Adam          *16c*

Smith would be disappointed in the way his economic theories have been used—and

misused.

## EXERCISE 17-1    Appropriate language: Guided practice

A.  The writer of the following paragraph used language that is too informal for the audience—an educated group of nonexperts. Revise the paragraph by replacing slang, regional expressions, nonstandard English, and sexist language. The numbers in the margin refer to appropriate rules in section 17 of *Rules for Writers,* Sixth Edition. The first revision has been done for you, and a suggested revision of this exercise appears in the back of the book.

                *Englishman*
In the 1800s, an ~~English dude~~ named Thomas Robert Malthus became involved     *17d*

in economics. He was really psyched about predicting how many more people would     *17d*

populate the world eventually and how much food would be available for them. What

he figured out was gross. He said people kept having children faster than men could     *17d, 17f*

produce enough to feed them. There was no way to avoid it. Hard times and wars

would do most people in. According to Malthus, famine, plagues, and even wars     *17d*

were necessary to knock off some excess people so the remainder could have enough     *17d*

food.

B.  The writer of the following paragraph used too much puffed-up language for an audience of educated nonexperts. Revise the paragraph, replacing jargon, pretentious language, and sexist language. Rule numbers in the margin refer to appropriate rules in section 17 of *Rules for Writers,* Sixth Edition. The first revision has been done for you, and a suggested revision of this exercise appears in the back of the book.

                       *population grows faster than food supplies.*
Robert Malthus proved that ~~the progression of population is exponential while~~     *17b*

~~the amplification of foodstuffs proceeds mathematically.~~ His cerebrations led him to     *17b*

oppose any help for economically deprived people. He believed that by relieving the     *17b*

immediate problems of the poor, the government actually made it harder for every-

one to feed his family. Malthus said that if the government subsidized their basic     *17f*

needs, people would only have more children, thus increasing the population even

more. Then the inevitable famine or drought would have to eliminate even more

people to facilitate the survival of a few. Everyone from worker to foreman was     *17a, 17f*

caught in the same predicament. It is no wonder that when the English historian

Thomas Carlyle finished reading Malthus's theories, he pronounced economics "the

dismal science."

**EXERCISE 17-2**    **Appropriate language**    To read about this topic, see section 17
in *Rules for Writers*, Sixth Edition.

Change the italicized words and phrases in the following sentences to more appropriate language
for an educated audience of nonexperts. Consult the dictionary if necessary. Do not change the
meaning of a sentence. Example:

*could not improve*

David Ricardo was another nineteenth-century economist who thought people ~~had to stay put in~~
*their social position.*                                                    ^
~~their social class.~~
^

1.  Ricardo and Malthus were t*ight, close buddies*, but they argued constantly.

2.  They did agree on one thing: The future looked *inauspicious* for humanity.

3.  Ricardo didn't *figure it all out* just by calculating population growth.

4.  He accumulated statistical *corroboration* for the validity of his theory of economics.

5.  His theory predicted that workers would always be *lowest on the totem pole*, that industri-
    alists would barely be able to *hang in there*, and that landowners would always be wealthy
    and powerful.

6.  His theory made the landowners the *bad guys*.

7.  In those days, landowners were called "landlords"; they rented land to tenant *agriculturists*.

8.  Landlords collected rents; but since their land also supplied food for the country, they held
    *humongous* power.

9.  Landlords would *as lief* die as give up their power.

10. When landlords *upped* land-rent fees, workers had to pay more for bread and the industri-
    alists had to pay higher wages without getting any increase in production.

## EXERCISE 17-3    Appropriate language    To read about this topic, see section 17
in *Rules for Writers*, Sixth Edition.

Circle the letter of the more appropriately worded sentence in each pair. Assume an educated audience of nonexperts, and be prepared to explain your choices. Example:

   a. **Malthus did not come up with any suggestions for ameliorating the lot of the common man.**

   (b.) **Malthus did not suggest any way to make life better for ordinary people.**

1a.  Malthus opposed loans to the poor because he did not believe poor families would ever have enough income to deal with negative savings.

 b.  Malthus opposed loans to the poor because he saw no way for poor people to increase their income enough to pay off debts.

2a.  Every member of society found that his life was impacted by Malthus's "laws" and their parameters.

 b.  No one escaped the consequences of Malthus's "laws": Rich and poor both suffered the consequences of overpopulation.

3a.  Malthus saw hope only in limiting marriages; he believed that if marriages were restrained, there would be fewer eventual workers and wages would go up.

 b.  The one bright idea Malthus had was to put a brake on marriages; fewer weddings meant fewer kids and eventually fewer workers and higher wages.

4a.  Ricardo said that the value added to a product by a man's labor was often greater than the wages paid to the laborer.

 b.  Ricardo said that the value workers added to a product was not reflected in the workers' wages.

5a.  In Ricardo's view, there was no viable system workers could utilize to improve their lot; they would always be stuck between a rock and a hard place.

 b.  Ricardo said that workers had almost no hope of improving their lives.

## EXERCISE 17-4    Appropriate language: Guided review

Revise the following paragraph using standard English free of slang, jargon, pretentious language, and sexist language. The numbers in the margin refer to appropriate rules in section 17 of *Rules for Writers*, Sixth Edition. The first sentence has been revised for you.

~~The relation between the~~ *The* theories of economists Thomas Malthus and David Ricardo ~~is associative rather than causal.~~ *show certain similarities, but one did not cause the other.* Their visions of the future are similar, but     *17a*

each arrived at his conclusions on his own. Ricardo predicted a dreary future; he

said that future workers would not have enough bread to buy bread. It was not ex-     *17d*

actly the same picture Malthus painted, but it was equally dismal. A modern

scholar, Robert Heilbroner, once said that these two men "changed the world from

an optimistic to a pessimistic one." Before them, most people believed that the world

would just naturally get phatter. After them, the natural world seemed to be an en-     *17d*

emy of the world's people. Although both Malthus and Ricardo studied the problem,

neither of them could render intelligible the reasons for the recurring fluctuations in     *17b*

the country's economic well-being. Nor could any other economist who offered his     *17f*

theories on the subject. Malthus and Ricardo saw only a gloomy image of future life.

Scrupulously honest, they reported that vision but offered no solutions to the prob-

lems they predicted. For many people, economics continues to be a dismal attempt

to elucidate the reasons for behavior of phenomena in the market.     *17b*

# EXERCISE 18-1    Exact words: Guided practice

In the following paragraph, improve word choices by replacing general words with specific ones and revising clichés and mixed figures of speech. Be sure that connotations are appropriate, that idioms are used properly, and that words are not misused. The numbers in the margin refer to appropriate rules in section 18 of *Rules for Writers*, Sixth Edition. The first revision has been done for you, and a suggested revision of this exercise appears in the back of the book.

                                   *dominated*

Economics is not totally ~~domineered~~ by men. Even in the 1800s, when Thomas     *18c*

Malthus and David Ricardo were the experts, one leading writer about economics

was a woman, Jane Marcet. Marcet wrote for the popular press. One of her favorite

things to write about was political economy. In her book *Conversations in Political*     *18b*

*Economy,* Marcet summarized economic doctrines before 1800. Her aim was differ-

ent than that of either Malthus or Ricardo. Rather than propounding a new theory     *18d*

of her own, she was happy as a lark to popularize theories of other people.     *18e*

Twentieth-century women have done more than write about theories that men have

proposed. Some of them have taken the bull by the horns and charged full steam     *18f*

ahead. Sally Herbert Frankel, for example, made the first official calculations of the

Union of South Africa's national income. She is only one of the increasing number

of ladies who make careers in economics.     *18a*

**EXERCISE 18-2**     **Exact words**     To read about this topic, see section 18 in *Rules for Writers*, Sixth Edition.

A. In each of the following sentences, circle the more specific word or phrase in parentheses. Example:

Alice Mitchell Rivlin was an important (person/(economist)) in the federal government.

1. Rivlin worked for (an important government office/the US Congressional Budget Office), where she (secured an important position/became director of that office).

2. She received her BA from (Bryn Mawr College/a prestigious eastern women's college) and her (PhD/highest degree) from Radcliffe College.

3. Rivlin's first job, at (the Brookings Institution/a think tank) in Washington, DC, lasted (for some time/from 1957 to 1966).

4. Most of her (publications/books) have been (put out/published) by the Brookings Institution.

5. Rivlin's interest in government finances carried over into the educational world when she became (a teacher/a professor of public policy) at (George Mason University near Washington, DC/a university in northern Virginia).

B. Edit the following sentences to correct inappropriate connotations. (See a thesaurus, the Glossary of Usage in *Rules for Writers*, Sixth Edition [p. 565], or a dictionary if necessary.) Example:

         *perceptive*
Alice Rivlin was ~~crafty~~ enough to understand the interrelatedness of individual budget items.
     ^

6. She planned to execute a thorough analysis of every part of the federal budget.

7. Rivlin did not claim that federal government services were cheap.

8. What she pushed was the idea that legislators should have easy access to information they needed.

9. She allowed herself no alibi for incomplete work.

10. Rivlin's work has proved conclusively that ladies can be extremely competent in financial matters.

**EXERCISE 18-3**    **Exact words**    To read about this topic, see section 18 in *Rules for Writers*, Sixth Edition.

A.  Circle the correct word or expression in parentheses. Example:

Alice Rivlin had the skill and (patients/(patience)) to analyze the federal budget; she (planned on doing/ (planned to do)) a thorough job.

1.  She wanted her work to have one specific (effect/affect), and she was determined to (try and/ try to) succeed.

2.  She planned (on making/to make) the budget, that (incredible/incredulous) mass of material, more available to Congress before Congress actually needed it.

3.  She had no (allusions/illusions) about the difficulty of the task; luckily for Congress, she proved (capable to do/capable of doing) it.

4.  When voting on the budget becomes (eminent/imminent/immanent), members of Congress need some (type of a/type of) clear, easy-to-understand document.

5.  That document must be easily (assessable/accessible) to any representatives who (plan on voting/plan to vote).

B.  Edit the following sentences to correct any misused words or idioms. Mark the one correct sentence "OK." (See 18c, 18d, the Glossary of Usage in *Rules for Writers*, Sixth Edition [p. 565], or a dictionary if necessary.) Example:

complement

The work of the Congressional Budget Office should ~~compliment~~ the work of Congress.
                                                  ^

6.  Members of Congress have been known to get very angry at a budget director whose work was not satisfactory.

7.  Sometimes the Budget Office must try and please a representative.

8.  The director of the Budget Office, however, must maintain that office's independents from members of Congress.

9.  Perhaps Alice Rivlin's style was different than that of some other budget officers, for she got the job done without making too many enemies.

10. In fact, Rivlin's performance at the Budget Office may account for her becoming deputy director of the Office of Management and Budget in 1993.

**EXERCISE 18-4**     **Exact words**     To read about this topic, see section 18 in *Rules for Writers*, Sixth Edition.

---

Edit the following sentences to delete or replace clichés and to clarify mixed figures of speech. Mark the two correct sentences "OK." Example:

> *be undertaking too much*
> Would an economist ~~bite off more than she could chew~~ if she tried to find out why better financial
>     ^          *fail to materialize?*
> rewards for women so often ~~hang fire?~~
>                            ^

1. Rivlin has had more than one iron in the fire; besides her budget work, she has written several books and taught public policy at George Mason University.

2. Rivlin did not sweep problems under the rug to take root there and come unraveled; she dealt with them before they became bigger problems.

3. When Rivlin was chosen as a MacArthur Foundation fellow, it was crystal clear that her talents and dedication had been recognized.

4. Rivlin is not the only modern woman to choose economics for her specialty.

5. Looking for such women is no longer like hunting for a needle in a haystack.

6. It goes without saying that women's roles in the labor market have changed radically.

7. It is a crying shame that the economic status of women has not kept pace with these changes. Why?

8. She may be playing with fire, but Cynthia Lloyd wants to get her feet wet dealing with that question.

9. In so doing, she has made the study of women in the labor market an integral and accepted part of economic analysis.

10. Her studies don't claim that money grows on trees but ask why women's efforts to get their share are always put on the back burner.

## EXERCISE 18-5    Exact words: Guided review

Edit the following paragraph for language appropriate for an audience of educated nonexperts. The numbers in the margin refer to appropriate rules in section 18 of *Rules for Writers*, Sixth Edition. The first revision has been done for you; find and correct the other five problems.

              *from*

Women economists have been no different ~~than~~ men economists in the range of     18d

their interests. Jane Marcet was interested in writing about economics for the pop-

ular press, not in developing theories of her own. Cynthia Lloyd's primary concern

is for improved economic status for women in the labor market. Alice Rivlin stays   18e

busy as a bee as senior fellow in the economic studies program at the Brookings

Institution in Washington, DC. Sally Herbert Frankel's interest is finance, particu-

larly South African national income. Jane Jacobs concentrates on cities because she

believes they have a significance impact on national economies. She claims that only  18c

cities can maintain or effect a nation's economic life enough to cause real change.   18c

Phyllis Deane intends on studying developing countries. She keeps her shoulder to  18d, 18f

the wheel as she digs deep to find ways to understand the economies of these coun-

tries.

## REVIEW OF 16–18: Clarity (word choice)

Edit the following essay for problems with word choice. The numbers in the margin refer to appropriate rules in sections 16–18 of *Rules for Writers*, Sixth Edition. The first revision has been done for you.

Economics, ~~which is~~ a branch of social science, deals with the production, distribution, and consumption of goods and services. However, you'd better believe it's not an exact science, though economists strive to make it so.      *16e*   *17d*

Economists have several aggravating habits. One of the worst is the habit of "two-handedness." An economist will say, "On the one hand, interest rates may rise and . . ." In the next breath, he will say, "On the other hand, interest rates may fall and . . ." Harry Truman used to get angry at advisers who talked like that. He once said that what he really needed was a one-handed economist.      *18c*   *17f*   *18d*

If the current volume of *Who's Who in Economics* fell off its library shelf, the floor would be dented by this 935-page book. Hundreds of names are in that volume, but the same few keep rising to the top and surfacing. Whenever people discuss economics, they nearly always refer to Malthus, Ricardo, Veblen, or last but not least Keynes. But the same name nearly always heads the list. Just as cream always rises to the top of the ladder of success, Adam Smith's name has led all the rest for two centuries.      *16b*   *16a*   *18e*   *18f*

Pretend you are the host of a current TV show about money. Pretend also that you write books with titles like *The Money Game* and *Supermoney*. What type of a name would you choose for your *nom de plume*? You would want an easily recognized name. You might do just what George Jerome W. Goodman did when he started a successful TV show about managing money: He called himself "Adam Smith."      *18d*   *18b*

## EXERCISE 19-1    Fragments: Guided practice

Edit the following paragraphs to eliminate sentence fragments. The numbers in the margin refer to appropriate rules in section 19 of *Rules for Writers*, Sixth Edition. The first revision has been done for you, and a suggested revision of this exercise appears in the back of the book.

*Four*
~~How four~~ young Englishmen added a word to the world's vocabulary in the     19a
^
1960s. A word that became synonymous with the 1960s. Especially with the music     19b, 19c
of that time. That word was, of course, "Beatles." The Beatles became the most famous popular musical group of the twentieth century. And held the loyalty of many     19c
fans into the next century.

The Beatles were popular in Liverpool, England, and in Hamburg, Germany.
Before they came to America on tour and became world famous. Liverpool and     19a
Hamburg loved the four young men and their music. The Beatles' favorite club was
the Cavern in Liverpool. Where they hung out together, played day and night, and     19c
attracted many fans. A Liverpool disc jockey first called attention to them, and a
Liverpool music critic and record store owner became their first manager. The disc
jockey called them "fantastic." Saying that they had "resurrected original rock 'n'     19b
roll." The music critic who became their manager, Brian Epstein, made them shape
up as a group. Promoting them, arranging club dates for them, and badgering record     19b
companies for them. He was determined to win a recording contract for this exciting new group.

In England, the record buying led to the publicity. In America, the publicity led
to the record buying. Everyone wanted copies of the original singles. "Love Me Do,"     19c
"Please, Please Me," and "From Me to You." In America, audiences made so much
noise that no one could hear the music. Crowds of screaming teenagers surrounded
the Beatles wherever they went. Determined to touch one or more of these famous     19b
music makers. Reporters observing the conduct of fans at Beatles' concerts found
that they had to invent another word. To describe the wild, almost insane behavior     19b
of the fans. They called it "Beatlemania."

**EXERCISE 19-2**    **Fragments**    To read about this topic, see section 19 in *Rules for Writers*, Sixth Edition.

---

Each of the following word groups includes a subordinating word. One word group in each pair contains a fragment. Write "OK" after each complete sentence and "frag" after each fragment. Example:

   a. John Lennon lived with his Aunt Mimi until he was grown. Because his parents had separated and his mother had given John to Mimi.   *frag*

   b. His father took him from Mimi when John was about five. Because his mother returned him to Mimi, he grew up as Mimi's child.   *OK*

1a. When John Lennon was a teenager, his mother, Julia, began to pay attention to him.

  b. When Julia, John Lennon's mother, bought him a guitar and let him stay with her instead of his Aunt Mimi.

2a. Although he studied art in college, he soon became more interested in music.

  b. Although Julia encouraged his music and put up with the boyish pranks that annoyed Aunt Mimi.

3a. His mother died before he was full grown. While John was still in college, in fact.

  b. Mimi's husband, his uncle, had died while John still lived with them.

4a. John asked Paul McCartney to join his group, and later Paul brought in George Harrison, and all three asked Ringo Starr to join them. Before they cut their first record.

  b. In their early days, the Beatles copied people like Elvis Presley and Little Richard. Before these English boys even visited America, they sang with American accents.

5a. The Beatles gave one reason for quitting their tours in 1966. That the tours were wrecking their playing.

  b. Stopping the tours gave the Beatles an opportunity to expand their talents. That they learned to read musical notes and write their own music was key to their improvement as musicians.

**EXERCISE 19-3**    **Fragments**    To read about this topic, see section 19 in *Rules for Writers*, Sixth Edition.

---

Underline each fragment in the following paragraphs. (Consult the chart on p. 149 of *Rules for Writers*, Sixth Edition, if necessary.) Do not correct the errors, but be prepared to discuss possible revision strategies for each fragment. The first fragment is underlined for you.

Paul McCartney wrote many of the Beatles' songs. A good student who learned quickly, he began composing songs when he was about fourteen.

Paul said that sometimes a song just came to him, like "Eleanor Rigby." One of his most famous and moving songs. The song is about a lonely woman who can't connect with other people. Paul was sitting at the piano not working on anything special. Just fooling around with melodies and rhythms. Then some notes played themselves in his head and so did some words. Like "Daisy Hawkins picks up the rice in the church where a wedding has been." Later Paul saw the name "Rigby" on a shop in Bristol. And decided he liked that name better than "Hawkins," especially with "Eleanor" instead of "Daisy." He and John Lennon finished the song together.

Paul wrote "Hey, Jude" in an effort to help John's son, Julian, who was upset over his parents' separation. Paul wanted the boy not to be sad. "To take a sad song and make it better." He decided to change "Julian" to "Jude" after he finished the song. Because he wanted the song to have a country-and-western feel.

All of the Beatles wrote songs, and often they collaborated on one, but Paul McCartney and John Lennon wrote most of the songs the Beatles sang.

**EXERCISE 19-4**     **Fragments**     To read about this topic, see section 19 in *Rules for Writers*, Sixth Edition.

---

Correct the fragments in the following paragraphs. The first revision has been done for you. Find and revise ten more fragments.

                         *his*

George Harrison was known in school for two things~~,~~ ~~His~~ sharp clothes and his love of the guitar. His mother said he sometimes practiced the guitar for hours. Not stopping until his fingers were bleeding. When George met John Lennon, he found another guitar lover. Although they went to the same school, they did not meet there. Because George was two years younger and they had no classes together. Instead, they met on the school bus. After they became friends, they spent most of their time at George's house, playing their guitars.

When George, John, Paul McCartney, and Ringo Starr formed a group, the four experimented with all kinds of things. From melodies and sounds to drugs. George, however, began to want more out of life. To find answers to the big questions he had about war and loneliness and reasons for living. The others agreed to search with him, and George Harrison became their guide.

Later, George and his wife went to India. Where a religious festival they attended impressed them deeply. When George returned to England, he read many books about meditation. And went to hear Indian holy teachers. He shared what he read and heard with the other Beatles. Who were just as interested as George was. When George learned that a holy man called the Maharishi was going to speak on transcendental meditation, he told his friends. They all went to listen to him. To learn whatever they could that would help them.

The Beatles were headed in a new direction. A direction that was obvious in their next album, *Sgt. Pepper's Lonely Hearts Club Band.* The album had innovative lyrics and an amazing musical background. A forty-one-piece orchestra, guitar, sitar, doubled voices, a comb-and-paper instrument, and all kinds of electronic and percussion tricks. The Beatles were no longer copycat rock 'n' rollers.

**EXERCISE 19-5**   **Fragments**   To read about this topic, see section 19 in *Rules for Writers*, Sixth Edition.

---

Half of the following word groups are complete sentences. The other half contain fragments. Correct the fragments, and mark the complete sentences "OK." Example:

> As a child and a teenager, Ringo Starr spent a total of three years in the hospital/ ~~Because~~ *because* of two severe health problems.

1.  When Ringo Starr was six, a burst appendix put him in the hospital for a whole year. Because of problems the rupture caused.

2.  Doctors had to perform several operations; Ringo could not attend school at all that year.

3.  His babysitter taught him to read and write, so he did not fall too far behind in his school-work.

4.  When he was thirteen, Ringo had to go back into the hospital. And stay there for two years while doctors treated a lung condition.

5.  Now fifteen, he worked at various jobs. But what he really liked best was playing the drums for his many fans.

6.  Teaching himself on drums he bought on the installment plan, he played with different musical groups in Liverpool, including the Beatles.

7.  When Ringo joined the Beatles, not everyone was sure that he could handle the job. For example, George Martin, who invited them to London to record.

8.  Martin insisted on a standby drummer as insurance. Someone ready to step in just in case Ringo was not good enough.

9.  Ringo's many devoted fans were not surprised when he handled the job and became a full-fledged Beatle, making new friends at every engagement.

10. Many people considered him the most likable member of the group. Because of his easy smile and his open approach to life.

## EXERCISE 19-6    Fragments: Guided review

Find and correct the sentence fragments in the following paragraphs. The numbers in the margin refer to appropriate rules in section 19 of *Rules for Writers*, Sixth Edition. The first revision has been done for you.

Many people influenced the Beatles in their career. For example, Bob Waller, a disc jockey in Liverpool,/. He first called attention to them in one of his articles. "They resurrected original rock 'n' roll," he wrote. When he first heard them in 1961. From Stu Sutcliffe, a talented musician who sometimes played with them, the Beatles copied several things. Their hairstyle, their dress, and much of their philosophy. George Martin, who produced their records, advised them how to improve after their early records. And taught them how to use tapes.    19c  19a  19c  19c

The person who influenced them most, however, was Brian Epstein. Owner of some record stores and reviewer of new records. When a customer asked for a record by a group Epstein had never heard of, he went from club to club. Looking for a group calling itself "The Beatles." By the end of 1961, he had become the group's manager. Convinced that he had found talented and original musicians. His contract said that he was to promote the Beatles and arrange their tours and club dates. His other duty was really the most important. To get record contracts for them.    19b  19b  19b  19b

Epstein did far more than his contract called for. He made the young men wear suits every time they performed. Until their gray, collarless outfits became a symbol of the Beatles. He made another demand of them. That they be on time for appearances. He even made them quit chewing gum on the stage. And by the time he had done all these things, he had also gotten them a recording date. Why were the Beatles so devastated by Epstein's death? When Brian Epstein was found dead of an accidental drug overdose in 1967. The Beatles lost far more than a good manager. They lost a close friend and mentor.    19a  19a  19a

## EXERCISE 20-1     Run-on sentences: Guided practice

Edit the following paragraphs to eliminate run-on sentences. Each rule number in the margin indicates a problem and suggests an effective method of revision. See section 20 of *Rules for Writers*, Sixth Edition. The first revision has been done for you, and a suggested revision of this exercise appears in the back of the book.

Have you ever heard of the Wobblies ?̷ Not~~not~~ many people have these days. That's          *20c*

a shame they did at least two things for which they should be remembered. They          *20d*

probably saved the labor movement in America, they definitely gave American folk          *20a*

music some of its most unforgettable songs. No one really knows how they got their

nickname almost everyone knows a song or two that they inspired.          *20a*

The Wobblies were the members of the Industrial Workers of the World (IWW),

this union was a small but militant coalition of radical labor groups. The Wobblies          *20d*

could not get along with the major union groups of the day, in fact, they alienated          *20b*

most of those groups.

The major unions disliked the Wobblies immensely, nevertheless they learned          *20d*

some valuable lessons from them. The first lesson was to avoid getting involved in

politics. If there was one thing the Wobblies hated more than capitalism, it was pol-

itics. The Wobblies avoided politics for one good reason, they believed that political          *20b*

affiliation caused the death of unions. What else did the major unions learn, they          *20c*

learned to deal realistically with workers' problems. Major unions also learned new

recruiting techniques from the Wobblies. In addition, they copied the Wobblies in de-

voting their energy to nuts-and-bolts issues affecting the workers.

The major unions never recognized their debt to the Wobblies, the debt was still          *20a*

there for historians to see. Historians began to compile the story of the American la-

bor unions, then they finally recognized the contributions of the Wobblies.          *20d*

**EXERCISE 20-2**    **Run-on sentences**    To read about this topic, see section 20 in *Rules for Writers*, Sixth Edition.

One sentence in each of the following pairs is a run-on sentence. Find and correct the error, using an effective revision strategy. Mark the correct sentence "OK." Example:

> *Although*
> a. Joe Hill may not have been the first martyr of the labor movement, ~~however,~~ he was certainly its
>    ^
>    most skillful worker with words and music.
>
> b. Before his arrest in 1914 for killing a grocer in Salt Lake City, Joe Hill was simply the Swedish
>    immigrant Joseph Hillstrom; no one knew or cared much about him.    *OK*

1a. Ralph Chaplin was the only person who wrote anything about Joe Hill before Hill's execution, he jotted down just a few notes based on an interview with a drunken sailor.

  b. Serious historical research has not confirmed or denied those notes because researchers have turned up quite different stories.

2a. All the evidence introduced at Hill's trial was circumstantial; furthermore, the dead man's son, who had witnessed the murder, refused to identify Hill as the gunman.

  b. Did the state hide evidence it certainly seemed that way.

3a. One Wobbly told the police that he had been with Joe Hill in another location on the night of the murder, he also told a detective he could prove Hill's innocence.

  b. That man was promptly arrested and held in jail for the duration of the trial.

4a. At the end of the trial, the man was released and ordered to get out of the state.

  b. Hill's own attorneys did not do much to help him their attitude was as negative as that of the prosecutors.

5a. Because of their negative attitude, Hill discharged both of the attorneys who were supposed to be defending him.

  b. "I have three prosecutors here, I intend to get rid of two of them," he said.

6a. The state never showed a motive for the murder; furthermore, much evidence that Hill's attorneys could have used was never introduced.

  b. How did Hill get that bullet wound in his chest, he told the doctor he had gotten it in a fight over a woman.

7a. The doctor who treated Hill was not asked to testify about medical aspects of the case, as a matter of fact, his testimony would probably have prevented Hill's conviction.

b. Protests about Hill's conviction came from all over the world, but they were ignored.

8a. Important political figures tried to help Hill, hoping until the last minute that they could save him.

b. The Swedish consul pleaded for him, President Wilson sent telegrams to the governor of Utah.

9a. Legend has it that Hill's last words before the firing squad were "Don't mourn for me; organize," in fact, he said, "Yes, aim! Let her go! Fire!"

b. If Joe Hill is known at all today, it is probably because of Joe Glazer, his guitar, and the song "Joe Hill."

10a. Glazer was not the composer of "Joe Hill" its composers were Earl Robinson and Alfred Hayes.

b. Glazer, however, made the song known across America, singing it at banquets as well as on picket lines.

**EXERCISE 20-3    Run-on sentences**    To read about this topic, see section 20 in *Rules for Writers*, Sixth Edition.

Correct each run-on sentence using the method of revision suggested in brackets. Example:

> *with whom*
> From his death cell, Joe Hill sent a letter to Big Bill Haywood, he had worked ~~with Haywood~~ in the
>                                                                                    ^
> early days of the IWW. [*Restructure the sentence; see 20d.*]

1.  Joe Hill's final letter to Big Bill Haywood had only five sentences, it contained one line about his death, one admonition to Haywood, and three comments related to Hill's burial. [*Use a colon; see 20b.*]

2.  He commented briefly about his death he said, "I die like a true rebel." [*Restructure the sentence; see 20d.*]

3.  Hill told Haywood, "Don't waste time mourning for me, organize instead." [*Use a semicolon; see 20b.*]

4.  Hill, in prison in Utah, did not want to be buried in that state, he asked Haywood to haul his body into Wyoming, a hundred miles away. [*Use a coordinating conjunction; see 20a.*]

5.  Hill gave only one reason for requesting burial in Wyoming, he said, "I don't want to be found dead in Utah." [*Make two sentences; see 20c.*]

6.  On the night before his execution, he wrote a final poem, in it he made two requests. [*Restructure the sentence; see 20d.*]

7.  He wanted his body to be cremated, he wanted his ashes to be allowed to blow freely around the earth. [*Use a coordinating conjunction; see 20a.*]

8.  Here's how he said it in his poem,

    Let the merry breezes blow
    My dust to where some flowers grow.
    Perhaps some fading flower then
    Would come to life and bloom again. [*Use a colon; see 20b.*]

9.  Obviously, Joe Hill was not a great poet, however, he was clever with rhymes. [*Use a semicolon; see 20b.*]

10. Even in his will he managed to fit in a humorous rhyme,

    This is my last and final will.
    Good luck to all of you.
                    —Joe Hill [*Use a colon; see 20b.*]

**EXERCISE 20-4     Run-on sentences     **To read about this topic, see section 20 in *Rules for Writers*, Sixth Edition.

---

Revise each of the following run-on sentences in the way you think is most effective. Example:

**Joe Hill was not buried in Utah⁀he was not buried in Wyoming either.**

1. After Joe Hill's death, his body was sent to Chicago, a large auditorium was secured for the funeral services.

2. More than thirty thousand people overflowed the auditorium, they jammed the streets as they followed the funeral train to the cemetery.

3. Very few of these mourners knew Joe Hill personally, nevertheless, he was a true hero to them.

4. On that Thanksgiving Day of 1915, they knew that other people mourned him too they heard eulogies to him in nine different languages.

5. Those mourners and thousands like them sang his songs, because they did, Joe Hill's name lived on.

6. Hill's satirical, angry songs often had a surprising tenderness, it is no wonder that he was named poet laureate of the Wobbly movement.

7. In some ways, Joe Hill's death freed him, in other ways, he remains a prisoner.

8. Joe Hill did get part of his deathbed wish, his body was cremated.

9. He was cremated at the cemetery afterward his ashes were put in thirty envelopes and sent all over the world.

10. The IWW kept one envelope, the Department of Justice confiscated it in 1918 for use in a trial. Since the envelope was never returned, part of Joe Hill is still "in prison."

## EXERCISE 20-5     Run-on sentences: Guided review

Revise each run-on sentence in the following paragraphs, using the method of revision suggested by the rule number in the margin. See section 20 of *Rules for Writers*, Sixth Edition. The first sentence has been revised for you.

> *Although he*
> ~~He~~ never calls them by name, John Steinbeck immortalizes the Wobblies in *The*                    *20d*
> ^
> *Grapes of Wrath*. The novel is about the life of the Joad family. The Joads have lost              *20d*
> their farm during the Depression, the family has come to California seeking work.
> There is no permanent work for anyone, moreover, the money earned by picking          *20b*
> crops is not enough to feed the family.

Union organizers have talked to the workers about organizing and striking.
Tom, the oldest Joad son, has listened to them, however, he has not yet joined them.          *20a*
Tom is in hiding because he has accidentally killed a man in a fight. He spends all
his daylight hours alone, he has lots of time to think about his family's situation.          *20a*
Tom becomes convinced that life is unfair for his people, he decides to leave the fam-          *20d*
ily, find the union men, and work with them.

He is inarticulate when he tries to explain to Ma what he hopes to do he gropes          *20c*
for words to express his frustration and his hope. Ma asks him how she will know
about him, she worries that he might get killed and she would not know. Tom's re-          *20a*
assurances are almost mystical: "Wherever they's a fight so hungry people can eat,
I'll be there an' when our folks eat the stuff they raise an' live in the houses they
build, I'll be there."

If Tom had had a copy of the Wobblies' "little red song book," he could have
found less mystical words. Every copy of the book contained the Wobblies' Preamble,
the first sentence in the Preamble was unmistakably clear "The working class and          *20d, 20b*
the employing class have nothing in common." Tom would have understood those
words he would have believed them too.          *20b*

## EXERCISE 21-1    Subject-verb agreement: Guided practice

Circle the correct verb from each pair in parentheses. The numbers in the margin refer to appropriate rules in section 21 of *Rules for Writers,* Sixth Edition. The first selection has been made for you, and an answer to this exercise appears in the back of the book.

Before reaching college, nearly everyone already (knows / know) several facts    21e
about fables. Most students know, for example, that fables are short stories that
(conveys / convey) a moral. They also know that fables nearly always have animal    21i
characters but that animal characters alone (is / are) not a signal that the story is a    21h
fable. They know of Aesop, to whom most familiar fables in Western culture (is / are)    21b
attributed. They know that there (is / are) generally only two or three characters in    21g
an Aesop fable and that a crowd of observers almost never (has / have) a role in his    21f
stories.

Most adults recognize that the subject matter of Aesop's fables is nearly always
the same. Once in a while, but not often, politics (is / are) highlighted in a story.    21j
Usually, however, Aesop's fables point out the value of common sense or make gentle fun of human failings. Since neither foolish behavior nor human failings (seems /    21d
seem) to be in short supply, Aesop's stories keep on being told. Besides, they attract
a wide audience: Adults and children both (enjoy / enjoys) them. Everyone who has    21c
gone to school (is / are) supposed to know some of Aesop's fables. "The Fox and the    21e
Grapes," for instance, (is / are) familiar to many children as a story long before they    21k
understand its meaning.

## EXERCISE 21-2    Subject-verb agreement    To read about this topic, see section
21 in *Rules for Writers,* Sixth Edition.

Verbs in the following sentences are italicized. Underline the simple subject (or simple subjects) of each verb, and edit the sentence to make the subject and verb agree. Keep all verbs in the present tense. Do not change the three correct sentences. Example:

*have*
<u>Many</u> of the morals or wise sayings from fables ~~has~~ become a part of our language.
        ^

1. Phrases like "a wolf in sheep's clothing" *is used and understood* by many people.

2. The expression "a wolf in sheep's clothing" *comes* from one of Aesop's fables.

3. A flock of sheep and a hungry wolf *is* the main characters in the story.

4. After killing a sheep for their supper, the shepherd and his helpers *forgets* about the skin from the sheep.

5. The wolf, finding the discarded skin, *cover* himself with it.

6. Joining the flock, he *pretends* to be a mother looking for her lamb.

7. The flock *accept* him as a sheep.

8. Neither the sheep nor the shepherd *notice* the wolf at first.

9. Daily luring a lamb from the flock, the wolf *feeds* himself very well for a while.

10. Everyone hearing the story *understand* its warning to beware of people pretending to be what they are not.

## EXERCISE 21-3    Subject-verb agreement    To read about this topic, see section
21 in *Rules for Writers*, Sixth Edition.

All of the following sentences have two subjects and verbs (some of the subject-verb pairs are in subordinate structures). The simple subjects are italicized. Edit each sentence to make the subjects and verbs agree. Keep all verbs in the present tense. One subject-verb pair in each sentence is correct. Example:

> *is*
> "Sour grapes" ~~are~~ a common expression, but not everyone knows the origin of that phrase.
> ^

1. Aesop's *story* "The Fox and the Grapes" tells about a fox *who* try unsuccessfully to get some grapes.

2. There are a big *bunch* of grapes hanging over the top of a wall, and the *fox* is hot and thirsty.

3. A favorite *food* of his are grapes, and *he* leaps up to get some—without success.

4. Hoping that no *crowd* of friends are watching, the *fox* takes a running leap for the top of the wall.

5. Unsuccessful, the *fox* in the story tries again and again with the same result; neither his *cleverness* nor his high *leaps* is successful.

6. Embarrassed, the *fox* fears that *news* of his failures are going to give his friends something to tease him about.

7. The fox's *pride and* his *self-confidence* has suffered, so *he* claims not to want the grapes anyway.

8. The *fox,* stalking proudly off with his nose in the air, say that the *grapes* are sour.

9. *Everyone* know that the *fox* does not believe his own words.

10. To save their pride, *people* often pretends not to want what *they* cannot get.

## EXERCISE 21-4    Subject-verb agreement: Guided review

Circle the correct verb from each pair in parentheses. The numbers in the margin refer to appropriate rules in section 21 of *Rules for Writers*, Sixth Edition. The first selection has been made for you.

From one of Aesop's lesser-known fables (comes)/ come) the question "Who's going to bell the cat?" The fable "Belling the Cat" describes the long battle between mice and cats.    *21g*

In the story, a committee of many mice is appointed to find a way to keep the cat from killing so many mice. Everyone on the committee (tries / try) to solve the problem. There (is / are) many committee meetings and much discussion, but in the end neither the committee nor its chairperson (is / are) able to make any good suggestions. Finally, the time comes for the committee to make its report at a public meeting. Embarrassed, the committee (reports / report) its failure.    *21e*    *21g*    *21d*    *21f*

At first, there is only silence; no one wants to accept the committee's report as the final word on the problem. Then a little pip-squeak among the mice (suggests / suggest) tying a bell on the cat. The young mouse makes quite a speech in favor of his idea. According to that mouse, statistics (shows / show) that no mice have ever been captured by a noisy cat. The mouse points out that his solution would not cost much; a bell and a string (is / are) all the equipment needed to give the mice warning of the cat's approach. The mouse who makes the suggestion gets a round of applause. The committee members, who (wishes / wish) that they had thought of the idea, are silent. Then a wise old mouse asks, "Who will bell the cat?" The experienced mice and the young pip-squeak (is / are) silent.    *21b*    *21j*    *21c*    *21i*    *21c*

It is easy to make suggestions that other people (has / have) to carry out.    *21a*

## EXERCISE 22-1    Pronoun-antecedent agreement: Guided practice

Edit the following paragraphs for problems with pronoun-antecedent agreement. The numbers in the margin refer to appropriate rules in section 22 of *Rules for Writers*, Sixth Edition. The first revision has been done for you, and a suggested revision of this exercise appears in the back of the book.

Everyone has heard of Dorothy and Toto and their tornado "flight" from Kansas

to Oz. ~~They also know~~ *Everyone also knows* that the Oz adventure was pure fantasy and that it ended    22a

happily. But another girl from Kansas took real flights all around the real world.

Whenever she landed safely after setting one of her many records, everyone rejoiced

and sent their congratulations to her. When she disappeared on her last flight, the    22a

whole world mourned. Not every pilot can claim they have that kind of following.    22a

Neighbors knew that Amelia Earhart would not be a typical "lady." A child as

curious, daring, and self-confident as Amelia was bound to stand out among peers.

When she and her sister Muriel were young, girls were supposed to play with dolls.

If a girl played baseball or collected worms, they were called "tomboys" and were    22a

often punished. Boys and girls even had different kinds of sleds—the girls' sleds

were lightweight, impossible-to-steer box sleds.

But the Earhart family lived by their own rules. Amelia's father, whom she de-    22b

pended on for approval, bought Amelia the boys' sled she longed for. Many fast trips

down steep hills gave Amelia a foretaste of flying with the wind in her face.

The closest Amelia came to flying was on a homemade roller coaster. She and

her friends built it, using an old woodshed for the base of the ride. They started eight

feet off the ground and tried to sled down the slope without falling off. No one was

successful on their first attempt, but Amelia kept trying until she had a successful    22a

ride. Satisfied at last, she declared that the ride had felt "just like flying."

## EXERCISE 22-2    Pronoun-antecedent agreement    To read about this topic, see
section 22 in *Rules for Writers*, Sixth Edition.

Five of the following word groups contain a problem with pronoun-antecedent agreement. Mark
the correct sentences "OK," and edit the incorrect ones to eliminate the problem. Example:

> *Pilots*
> During World War I, Amelia Earhart listened to wounded pilots' tales of adventure. ~~A pilot~~ would de-
>                                                                                          ^
> scribe a particularly daring wartime adventure and joke about their ability to beat the odds.

1.  After World War I, Amelia Earhart took flying lessons. She learned quickly, but the lessons
    cost her most of her salary.

2.  She wanted those lessons, so she worked two jobs to pay for them: She clerked for the tele-
    phone company and drove a dump truck for a sand and gravel company.

3.  Members of her family pooled their funds to buy a gift—a little yellow biplane—for her
    twenty-fourth birthday celebration; it was the perfect gift.

4.  Amelia Earhart soon learned that when someone owns a plane, they need a lot of money.

5.  She sometimes executed dangerous maneuvers before her teacher was sure Amelia could
    handle it.

6.  At first everyone could not believe their eyes when she deliberately put her plane into a spin.

7.  Each spectator would gasp when they heard her cut the engine off in a spin.

8.  But Amelia Earhart repeatedly pulled the plane out of its spin and landed safely, delighting
    everyone.

9.  When an aviator wants to break records, they will work very hard.

10. Aviation record keepers had to make a new entry in the record books: They had seen Amelia
    Earhart fly 14,000 feet high.

## EXERCISE 22-3    Pronoun-antecedent agreement    To read about this topic, see
section 22 in *Rules for Writers*, Sixth Edition.

In each set of sentences, circle the letter of the sentence that has a problem with pronoun-antecedent agreement. Which of the other two sentences (both correct) do you prefer? Put a check mark next to that sentence. Example:

(a.) A college dropout often gets little respect for their choosing to leave school.

b. College dropouts often get little respect for their choosing to leave school.

✔  c. A college dropout often gets little respect for choosing to leave school.

1a. Not everyone who drops out of college ruins their life.

 b. Not all students who drop out of college ruin their lives.

 c. Not all college dropouts ruin their lives.

2a. Students sometimes discover that they don't like their chosen field.

 b. A student sometimes discovers that he or she doesn't like their chosen field.

 c. Students may lose interest in their chosen field.

3a. People like Amelia, who quit school to learn to fly, must be very sure of themselves.

 b. Someone like Amelia, who quit school to learn to fly, must be very sure of themselves.

 c. Someone like Amelia, who quit school to learn to fly, must be very sure of herself or himself.

4a. In their catalog, Columbia University offered a wide range of courses, but Flying Airplanes was not among them.

 b. Flying Airplanes was not among the wide range of courses offered in Columbia University's catalog.

 c. In its catalog, Columbia University offered a wide range of courses, but Flying Airplanes was not among them.

5a. Amelia Earhart became a dropout any university would be proud to claim.

 b. Amelia Earhart became one of those dropouts any university would be proud to claim as theirs.

 c. Amelia Earhart became a dropout all universities would be proud to claim.

## EXERCISE 22-4    Pronoun-antecedent agreement: Guided review

Edit the following paragraphs for problems with pronoun-antecedent agreement. The numbers in the margin refer to appropriate rules in section 22 of *Rules for Writers,* Sixth Edition. The first revision has been done for you.

When Amelia Earhart became the first woman to cross the Atlantic in a plane, she got no money; she did get a free ride, fame, and job offers. Not ~~every flier~~ *all fliers* would think these rewards were enough for their time and trouble on the trip, but Amelia Earhart was delighted with the whole experience. Afterward, a book she wrote about that flight brought her another first: a publisher, a shrewd business manager, and a husband—all in one man, George Putnam. (Putnam also understood her fierce independence—not every man would sign a prenuptial agreement saying their wife could have a divorce anytime she asked!)

    22a

    22a

The first national organization for "flying women," formed by Amelia Earhart and a friend, recruited their members in the belief that every woman should follow her own interest. After all, who had made the first solo flight from Honolulu to the United States? From Los Angeles to Mexico City? And from Mexico City to New Jersey? It was she, Amelia Earhart. No woman ever did more to prove that they could handle jobs traditionally reserved for men.

    22b

    22a

Amelia Earhart's last "first" was never completed. When she tried to become the first pilot to fly around the world at the equator, she disappeared somewhere over the Pacific. The government searched more than 265,000 miles of air and sea space, but they found nothing.

    22a

In 1994, fifty-seven years after Amelia Earhart's disappearance, twelve-year-old Vicki Van Meter became the youngest female pilot to fly across the Atlantic. She took off from Augusta, Maine, from the very spot where Amelia Earhart had started her flight across the Atlantic. When Van Meter landed safely in Glasgow, everyone offered their congratulations, and Van Meter felt a special kinship with her predecessor, Amelia Earhart.

    22a

## EXERCISE 23-1    Pronoun reference: Guided practice

Edit the following paragraphs to correct errors in pronoun reference. The numbers in the margin refer to appropriate rules in section 23 of *Rules for Writers*, Sixth Edition. The first revision has been done for you, and a suggested revision of this exercise appears in the back of the book.

George and Mary Jones lived in Memphis during the Civil War. They were sympathetic to the Union, but the city definitely favored the Confederates. ~~This~~ *Being caught in the middle* made the war years especially hard on them. They looked forward to a much better life after the war.                                                                              23b

At first, it seemed that they were going to have that better life. George got a job as a labor organizer, and Mary stayed at home to care for their four healthy children. Then came yellow fever. In nine months, Mary went from a happy wife and mother to a despondent widow that had no children. She had to find work. Because you must have some meaning for living, she needed work that she could care strongly about.                                                                              23e, 23d

By 1900, Mary had become involved in union activities all over the United States. She found her calling among the coal miners and their wives, a calling she followed for the next thirty years. Making friends with the workers and outwitting private detectives, she held secret meetings to help them organize and plan strategy.      23a
In the newspaper, it often reported her ability to outwit and outlast mine bosses and     23d
lawyers as well as to reawaken courage in disconsolate workers.

Mary Jones spent many nights in jail, but often her jailers did not know what to do with this attractive gray-haired woman whom the workers called "Mother." The jailers' confusion simply amused Mary, who was far more used to jail than they      23c
could imagine.

**EXERCISE 23-2**    **Pronoun reference**    To read about this topic, see section 23 in
*Rules for Writers,* Sixth Edition.

---

Six of the following sentences contain faulty pronoun references. Find the faulty references and
fix them. Mark the correct sentences "OK." Example:

> *and this job*
> Mother Jones got a job working in the textile mills, ~~which~~ made her conscious of how women work-
> ^
> ers were mistreated.

1. When Mother Jones started working in the textile mills at the turn of the century, she saw
   "the little gray ghosts," the child laborers which worked from sunup to sundown.

2. Children as young as six scooted along the floor oiling and cleaning the huge whirring
   looms, which often devoured a child's fingers or hand.

3. Mother Jones once led a delegation of three hundred children from Philadelphia to New York
   to dramatize their plight; in some of the newspapers they called her "the greatest female
   agitator in the country."

4. The speeches Mother Jones made about child labor were among her best: They called for
   legislation to forbid labor practices dangerous to children's health.

5. When Mother Jones asked for permission to bring three of the children to meet with
   President Theodore Roosevelt in New York, she was refused. It saddened her because she
   had hoped for the president's help.

6. Mother Jones asked again and was again refused. This second one saddened her even more,
   but she still did not consider the trip a failure.

7. She told the children and their parents that they had been successful.

8. Public awareness, which she felt would help the children, gradually began to increase.

9. Thousands of people had learned about the children's plight, which was bound to affect
   their thinking about child labor laws.

10. Mother Jones's optimism had another basis as well: The children would remember—and
    they would grow up.

**EXERCISE 23-3** **Pronoun reference** To read about this topic, see section 23 in
*Rules for Writers*, Sixth Edition.

---

Problem pronouns are italicized in the following paragraphs. Edit the paragraphs to eliminate
any misunderstandings these pronouns might cause. You may need to restructure some sentences. Example:

> *workers*
> In the mines, ~~you~~ didn't get much chance at the good life.
> ∧

Mother Jones was determined to change the intolerable working conditions in the mines.
After digging coal for twelve-to-fourteen-hour shifts, *they* found in their miners' pay envelopes
not US currency but scrip, paper money that was honored only by the mining company. Local
merchants had no use for the scrip, so *they* couldn't use it to buy food, clothes, or anything else.
Workers, therefore, had to rent their homes from the company and buy their supplies at company stores. In company-run schools, the workers' children were taught by teachers *that* were
hired by the company. *Their* families listened to company-paid ministers in company-owned
churches.

Songwriter Merle Travis may have broken a pronoun reference rule, but he certainly
summed *it* up neatly in one of his songs:

You load sixteen tons, what do you get?

Another day older and deeper in debt.

St. Peter, don't you call me 'cause I can't go,

I owe my soul to the company store.

[What pronoun does Travis use in a way that would be inappropriate in formal written English?]

## EXERCISE 23-4     Pronoun reference: Guided review

Edit the following paragraphs to correct errors in pronoun reference. The numbers in the margin refer to appropriate rules in section 23 of *Rules for Writers,* Sixth Edition. The first revision has been done for you.

Coal miners' struggles turned into actual war in the Kanawha Valley of West
Virginia, where ~~they~~ **miners** were striking. The mine owners dominated the courts and the     *23c*
newspapers; they did not need to worry about the law or public opinion. Although
the miners did not want to accept this, they were often forced to face it. Guards used     *23b*
violent tactics to maintain the mine owners' control, once spraying strikers' tent
colonies with machine-gun fire and kicking a pregnant woman so hard that her un-
born child died in the womb.

Mother Jones urged the miners to fight while she tried to gain the ear of the
governor, the federal lawmakers, and the public. In records of the fight, it says that     *23d*
two thousand miners came from outside the valley to help in the battle. The state
militia was called in, but the owners got control of the militia soon after it arrived.
En route to the state legislature to ask them for help, Mother Jones was kidnapped     *23c*
by soldiers, held incommunicado, put in solitary confinement, and tried by a military court. When the new governor of West Virginia, Henry D. Hatfield, investigated,
he found a soldier guarding an eighty-year-old pneumonia-ridden woman that had     *23e*
a 104-degree fever.

Word about the Kanawha situation got out, but Governor Hatfield acted first.
Out of his work came the Hatfield Agreement. This document, which historians of
the labor movement consider a major advance for workers in the United States,
forced the companies to recognize the union and to shorten the workday. Even more
important, it stipulated that companies must pay wages in US currency. He also     *23a*
guaranteed civilians the right to civil, not military, trials and dismissed all sentences
the military court had imposed—including the twenty-year prison term it had set for
Mother Jones.

## EXERCISE 24-1    Pronoun and noun case: Guided practice

Circle the correct pronoun from each pair in parentheses. The numbers in the margin refer to appropriate rules in section 24 of *Rules for Writers,* Sixth Edition. The first selection has been made for you, and an answer to this exercise appears in the back of the book.

When union organizer Mother Jones went to Colorado in 1913, no one worked harder than (she/her) to help the miners. (They/Them) and their families lived in    *24d, 24a* company houses that the company's own reports called unfit for human habitation. Although Mother Jones wanted to help the miners, she saw no way to get the two groups, the owners and (they/them), together.    *24c*

Mother Jones did not give up. When threatening posters went up all over town, she laughed and encouraged the miners with slogans like "(We/Us) miners have got    *24e* to stick together." When Mother Jones appealed to the governor for help, no one really expected the governor and (she/her) to agree, but many people hoped he    *24f* would help somehow. Instead, he simply ordered her out of the state.

The miners were evicted from their houses. (They/Them) and their families    *24a* moved into tents. After company guards raked the tents with machine-gun fire, the miners dug pits under the tents. The pits were deep enough to protect their families and (they/them) from gunfire, but at Ludlow, guards set fire to the tents. Whole    *24b* families were roasted to death in the pits. When word of the massacre got out, workers from all over the state swarmed to Ludlow. No one was ever as angry as (they/    *24d* them). They set fire to company buildings, fought the state and company troops, and took over the nearby mines and towns.

Mother Jones went to Washington to ask President Wilson for help. Although she and (he/him) did not agree on all points, he did establish a review board and    *24a* send in federal troops to restore order. The companies did not like the (president/    *24g* president's) sending in troops and absolutely refused to accept the findings of the review board. Eventually, the miners went back to work under almost the same conditions as before. Disappointed as they were, they knew that it was (she/her),    *24a* Mother Jones, who was the most disappointed of all.

## EXERCISE 24-2    Pronoun and noun case    To read about this topic, see section
24 in *Rules for Writers*, Sixth Edition.

Six of the following sentences have errors in pronoun or noun case. Find and fix the errors. Mark
"OK" next to the sentences that have no errors. Example:

> *he*
> **Mother Jones liked to discuss union affairs with her friend Terence Powderly; she and ~~him~~ could**
> ⌃
> **argue for hours about the best approach to a problem.**

1.  People all over the world knew about Mother Jones. Wherever she went, she was invited into
    their homes and their workplaces.

2.  Once when she was traveling with Fred Mooney in Mexico, a crowd stopped the train and
    urged Mooney and she to open the train window.

3.  Mooney and she were not sure whether they should open the window, but they decided to
    do so. When they did, she and him both were covered with red carnations and blue violets.

4.  Although the people gave the flowers to both him and her, the flowers were meant as gifts
    in honor of "Madre Yones."

5.  The trip to Mexico was exhausting, but it was she, over ninety, who never ran out of energy.

6.  When Mooney fretted about her health, it was her who laughed and proposed that they get
    on with their sightseeing.

7.  No one was more excited than her about the idea of a Pan-American Federation of Labor,
    an organization that would unite workers from Canada to South America.

8.  The president of Mexico was as pleased as her at the idea of bringing together all the work-
    ing people in the hemisphere.

9.  "This is the beginning of a new day for us working people," exclaimed Mother Jones.

10. It was a day Mother Jones long remembered; years later it brought happy smiles to she and
    her friends whenever they saw carnations and violets or thought of that day's events.

**EXERCISE 24-3**    **Pronoun and noun case**    To read about this topic, see section 24 in *Rules for Writers*, Sixth Edition.

Some of the personal pronouns in this passage are italicized; six of them are not in the correct case. The first one has been corrected for you. Find and correct the other five.

*she*
Though ~~her~~ and a friend would occasionally work together on the friend's campaign, Mother
∧
Jones avoided politics most of the time. *She*, the agitator, had no more interest in politics and political science than *her*, the labor organizer, had in economic theory. Mother Jones understood one kind of economics, the kind that dealt with wages, benefits, and the cost of bread and housing. The here-and-now problems of the poor called to Mother Jones so strongly that *she* had to do what *she* could to stop the injustice she saw around *her*.

Surprisingly, Mother Jones was not a supporter of woman suffrage. When the fight to win women's right to vote came along, it was not *her* who supported it. *Herself* and her people were the working classes, both men and women, and neither *she* nor *them* had much patience for the "society women" who led the movement. As far as Mother Jones was concerned, well-dressed women parading down the city streets carrying placards and banners did not help working men and women obtain a decent life. Mother Jones objected to *them* spending time and energy and money on activities that would not help her kind of people. Nor was *she* interested in helping a cause that would benefit only women; her concern was for all workers, regardless of gender. *She* seemed not to understand that the votes of the miners' wives might do as much to help the working men as *her* agitating and organizing did.

## EXERCISE 24-4    Pronoun and noun case: Guided review

Circle the correct pronoun from each group in parentheses. The numbers in the margin refer to appropriate rules in section 24 in *Rules for Writers*, Sixth Edition. The first selection has been made for you.

Eventually, labor organizer Mother Jones began to think about her death. She wrote her autobiography and made plans for her burial, but she could not have dreamed how her name would be kept alive many years after her death.

(She/ Her) and an editor friend began her autobiography when Mother Jones  24a
was ninety-two. Even with her friend working as hard as (she/her), Mother Jones  24d
found writing to be a grinding, demanding chore. Annoyed with her (friend/friend's)  24g
trying to make her remember details of her youth, she covered the first thirty years
of her life in a few paragraphs. She had trouble remembering even the later years,
confusing names and occasionally mixing up dates. She was never confused, however, about her conviction that working people were being unfairly treated. Nor did
she doubt the necessity for (she/her) and her friends to help redress the wrongs  24f
done to working people.

Mother Jones planned to be buried in a place special to her. Back in 1898, four
miners had been killed during a strike in Mount Olive, Illinois, and no cemetery in
town would allow the bodies of these men to be buried on its land. So the union
bought its own cemetery to bury them and others like them. For Mother Jones, burial in Miners Cemetery, Mount Olive, Illinois, was a way to say "(We/Us) working  24e
people have got to stick together" even after her death.

She would have been puzzled by a memorial honoring her work. In the mid-
twentieth century, some writers decided to publish a magazine devoted to exposing
fraud and injustice in society. (They/Them) and their friends named this new pub-  24a
lication *Mother Jones*. Mother Jones might not have appreciated the accolades it
won or its citation by the *American Journalism Review* as "best in the business for
investigative reporting," but she would have recognized at once the woman first
listed under the journal's masthead: "Mother Jones (1830–1930)—Orator, Union
Organizer, and Hellraiser."

## EXERCISE 25-1    *Who* and *whom*: Guided practice

Circle the correct pronoun from each pair in parentheses. The numbers in the margin refer to appropriate rules in section 25 of *Rules for Writers*, Sixth Edition. The first selection has been made for you, and an answer to this exercise appears in the back of the book.

Have you ever heard of George Leroy Parker? You probably have; you just don't think so because you don't know (who / whom) George Leroy Parker really was. He    *25a*
was born on a Utah ranch in 1867. There were several cowhands on the place, and some of them had other jobs as well. One or two did a bit of farming, others went in for gambling, and one was a horse thief and cattle rustler. Of them all, (who / whom)    *25b*
did young George find most attractive? George never had any question about (who /    *25a*
whom) he admired most on the ranch. (Who / Whom) else would it be but Mike, the    *25b*
horse thief and cattle rustler? George was so impressed by Mike that years later he would tell stories about Mike's exploits to (whoever / whomever) would listen. Mike    *25a*
was the man George was eternally grateful to because he taught George how to ride and shoot. George was so grateful, in fact, that he took that man's last name for his own. He wanted to honor Mike Cassidy, the man (who / whom) he admired above all    *25a*
others.

[*Note:* Sometimes the pronoun *whom* may be dropped without loss of clarity. Are there any *whom*s in this paragraph that you might choose to drop?]

**EXERCISE 25-2    *Who* and *whom***    To read about this topic, see section 25 in *Rules for Writers*, Sixth Edition.

_____

One sentence in each of the following pairs uses *who* and *whom* correctly and the other does not. Put "OK" after the correct sentence and correct the other one. Example:

    a. People who deliberately change their last names do so for specific reasons.    *OK*
                                                     *whom*
    b. Sometimes they are hiding from people ~~who~~ they have harmed.
                                                ^

1a. It is unusual for a man to change his last name to honor someone who he admires.

  b. George Leroy Parker became George Cassidy when he named himself for the man who had taught him the most.

2a. One day George said good-bye to Mike Cassidy, who was leaving for Mexico.

  b. The lawmen who Mike planned to outwit did not catch up with him this time.

3a. George decided to join up with whoever he could find to try a train robbery.

  b. He found the McCarty brothers and Matt Warner, to whom a robbery sounded like a good idea.

4a. The gang underestimated who they would be dealing with.

  b. The guard whom they threatened refused to open the safe.

5a. The gang then voted on whether to rob the passengers, whom they had not originally intended to disturb.

  b. The "no" votes won, so the gang left the passengers to wonder whom these vote-taking train robbers were.

[*Note:* Sometimes the pronoun *whom* may be dropped without loss of clarity. Are there any *whom*s in the preceding sentences that you might choose to drop?]

**EXERCISE 25-3**    *Who* and *whom*    To read about this topic, see section 25 in *Rules for Writers,* Sixth Edition.

---

Edit the following sentences to eliminate errors in the use of *who* and *whom.* Mark correct sentences "OK." Example:

> **George Cassidy, who was later known as Butch, robbed his first bank in 1889.**    *OK*

1. George Cassidy, who had already decided to rob the First National Bank of Denver, had a problem: Who could he find as a partner?

2. Maybe one of his old buddies who now lived in Star Valley, an almost perfect hideout, would be a partner on whom he could depend.

3. Whom else could it be but Tom McCarty, with whom George had tried his first train robbery?

4. When the robbers threatened the bank president with a bottle they said contained nitro-glycerin, others said it was only water. The bank president didn't know who to believe because he couldn't tell whom was lying.

5. Actually, it was water, but who could have been sure of that?

## EXERCISE 25-4    *Who* and *whom*: Guided review

Circle the correct pronoun from each pair in parentheses. The numbers in the margin refer to appropriate rules in section 25 of *Rules for Writers,* Sixth Edition. The first selection has been made for you.

George Cassidy got his nickname Butch from the people he served during one of the few times he earned an honest living. The people George Cassidy worked for from 1890 to 1892 knew him as an honest worker. The available records don't show (who/whom) trained him for his job—butchering sheep, hogs, and steers. (Whoever/ Whomever) had trained him had done it well. It was obvious to (whoever/ whomever) looked at his work that George Cassidy knew how to handle a knife. His customers, (who/whom) he may well have robbed later, were satisfied with his work. They probably did not realize how famous—or infamous—their butcher was to become. Even if Butch didn't know which townspeople had given him his name, obviously he liked it; he used it for the rest of his life. (Who/Whom) today hasn't heard of Butch Cassidy? (Who/Whom) did director George Roy Hill choose as the hero of one of his most popular films?

25a, 25a

25a

25a

25b

25b

## EXERCISE 26-1    Adjectives and adverbs: Guided practice

Edit the following paragraphs for correct use of adjectives and adverbs. The numbers in the margin refer to appropriate rules in section 26 of *Rules for Writers,* Sixth Edition. The first revision has been done for you, and an answer to this exercise appears in the back of the book.

Novelists have often used their storytelling talents to influence people's thinking. Charles Dickens did it in nineteenth-century England. From *David Copperfield*
to *Oliver Twist,* book after book depicted the plight of the poor and other ~~real~~ *really* unfor-      26a
tunate members of society. Harriet Beecher Stowe did it in nineteenth-century      26d
America, but with not hardly as many books. Her *Uncle Tom's Cabin* depicted
slavery so well that the book strongly influenced antislavery sentiments in the
decade before the Civil War.

Harriet Beecher Stowe considered slavery sinful and wanted her book to help
end slavery quick and peaceful. People first read parts of the novel ten years before      26a
the beginning of the war. An abolitionist magazine published it a few chapters at a
time, hoping the effect of the story would make readers feel so badly about slavery      26b
that they would rally to the abolitionist cause. Many people, reading *Uncle Tom's
Cabin* installment by installment, did become convinced that nothing could be
worser than living in slavery on a southern plantation.      26c

None of the abolitionists, who devoted their energy to abolishing slavery, expected a more perfect world when the book itself was published in 1852. But they      26c
certainly hoped that the book would be influential. It was. Of all the novels published that year, it was the best-seller on both sides of the Atlantic. Its popularity
was good news for the abolitionists. Harriet Beecher Stowe's wish came true.

## EXERCISE 26-2    Adjectives and adverbs    To read about this topic, see section 26
in *Rules for Writers*, Sixth Edition.

Both sentences in each of the following pairs are grammatically correct. The sentences mean different things because one uses an adjective, the other an adverb. Read both sentences carefully to understand their meaning. Then circle the letter of the sentence that answers the question and be prepared to explain what the other sentence means. Example:

**Which sentence means that southerners thought the book itself was dishonest?**

**(a.) Many southerners did not consider *Uncle Tom's Cabin* honest.**

**b. Many southerners did not consider *Uncle Tom's Cabin* honestly.**

1. In which sentence did the people do a poor job of judging?

    a.  Those people judged Mrs. Stowe's depiction of slave life inaccurate.

    b.  Those people judged Mrs. Stowe's depiction of slave life inaccurately.

2. Which sentence says that the slaves had trouble finding the escape routes?

    a.  Most slaves did not find their escape routes easy.

    b.  Most slaves did not find their escape routes easily.

3. In which sentence do northerners think Stowe herself was honest?

    a.  Most northerners believed Mrs. Stowe honest.

    b.  Most northerners honestly believed Mrs. Stowe.

4. In which sentence did the judges think that some people had more rights than others?

    a.  Southern judges did not consider all people equal.

    b.  Southern judges did not consider all people equally.

5. Which sentence says that the overseers were looking scared?

    a.  Rumors of escaping slaves made overseers look anxious when their slaves were out

        of sight.

    b.  Rumors of escaping slaves made overseers look anxiously when their slaves were

        out of sight.

**EXERCISE 26-3   Adjectives and adverbs**   To read about this topic, see section 26 in *Rules for Writers*, Sixth Edition.

Six of the adjectives and adverbs in the following paragraphs are not used correctly. The first one has been corrected. Find and correct the other five.

      *really*

 *Uncle Tom's Cabin* was ~~real~~ popular, even though it was a very long book. When it was published as a serial in the abolitionist magazine *National Era* in 1851 and 1852, people probably read all of it. But when the novel was published as a book, many people did not have enough time to read it. Since it had been a best-seller, enterprising publishers brought out new, abridged copies for more faster reading. By the end of the Civil War, many people knew the story of *Uncle Tom's Cabin* only from these shorter versions of it—both novels and plays.

 Unfortunately, their knowledge was not only incomplete; it was distorted. Publishers left out important sections of this most priceless story. For example, in the book, Uncle Tom works for three different owners, two of whom treat him fairly good. But in the shortened versions of the story, Tom works for only one owner, who treats him very cruel. Even insensitive readers rightly found that cruel owner, Simon Legree, vicious and judged all slave owners by that one. What had been a subplot in the novel—the story of George, Eliza, their baby, and the family's attempted escape to freedom in Canada—became a major portion of the story. Playwrights favored such dramatic subplots and incidents because they were easily dramatized.

 Modern readers are often real surprised when they read the entire novel, a book that American critic Edmund Wilson called "a much more remarkable book than one had ever been allowed to suspect."

**EXERCISE 26-4**   **Adjectives and adverbs: Guided review**

Edit the following paragraph for correct use of adjectives and adverbs. The numbers in the margin refer to appropriate rules in section 26 of *Rules for Writers*, Sixth Edition. The first revision has been done for you.

> Playwrights often find popular novels suitable for the stage. Produced as a play,
>
> *most successful*
> *Uncle Tom's Cabin* was the ~~successfulest~~ stage play of the 1800s. The play used only   26c
> ^
> the real dramatic portions of the novel and therefore somewhat slanted its basic   26a
>
> message. Even worse than the plays were the "Tom Shows" that toured small towns
>
> all over the North; these shows didn't have scarcely anything but the violent scenes.   26d
>
> Audiences felt very badly when they watched George and Eliza's desperate escape   26b
>
> over the ice with their baby. Dramatists played on their viewers' sympathy with the
>
> plight of this slave family. Viewers hoped until the very end that the family's escape
>
> would work out perfect. Distortion was bad in both the plays and the Tom Shows,   26a
>
> but it was worse in the Tom Shows, which turned this most unique story of slavery   26c
>
> in the South into little more than propaganda. Particularly moving scenes from the
>
> story continue to be used in plays and musicals. *The King and I* made use of
>
> several. If a modern movie is ever made from *Uncle Tom's Cabin*, the movie will no
>
> doubt reflect the same distortions present in the old plays and the Tom Shows—and
>
> will probably be just as popular.

## EXERCISE 27-1    Verb forms: Guided practice

Correct any nonstandard verb forms in the following paragraphs. The numbers in the margin refer to appropriate rules in section 27 of *Rules for Writers*, Sixth Edition. The first revision has been done for you, and an answer to this exercise appears in the back of the book.

       *don't*

Most Americans today ~~doesn't~~ realize that the American democratic system did     *27c*

        ^

not always include African Americans and women. The constitutional amendments

pass after the Civil War granted former slaves and all native-born African American     *27d*

men full voting rights, but the new amendments ignored women. Women had to wait

much longer—more than half a century—to be gave the right to vote.     *27a*

    Some individual states allowed women to vote as early as 1900, but by 1910

women activists decided to focus their energy on a federal amendment. When

Woodrow Wilson became president in 1913, women demonstrated along the inau-

guration route, marching and holding signs demanding the vote for women. Then in

1917, Alice Paul and a militant faction of the suffrage movement picketed the White

House and even chained themselves to fences. When they were threaten and at-     *27d*

tacked by male mobs, police ignored the men and arrested the women. In prison,

the women endured filthy cells, force-feeding when they gone on a hunger strike,     *27a*

and ill treatment. Some women was restrained for many hours in uncomfortable po-     *27a*

sitions with their arms high over their heads. One angry official repeatedly ask a     *27d*

doctor to declare one or more of the women insane. (The doctor refused.)

    President Wilson a man with major problems—a war abroad and women fight-     *27e*

ing for their rights at home. At first he tolerated the women picketers; he even send     *27a*

coffee out to them. Then he just wanted the women to lie down their signs and ban-     *27b*

ners and go home. But the increasing pressure from moderate and radical voices in

the movement as well as public outrage over the women's prison treatment finally

force Wilson to support a constitutional amendment for women's voting rights.     *27d*

**EXERCISE 27-2**    **Verb forms**    To read about this topic, see section 27 in *Rules for Writers*, Sixth Edition.

---

Edit the following paragraphs for missing *-ed* endings and incorrect forms of irregular verbs. The first revision has been done for you. You should make ten more.

      *led*
  Women who ~~leaded~~ the suffrage movement never used violence, but they thought of them-
      ^
selves as waging a war. They tried different strategies in different places and coordinated their

various attacks. Some concentrated on state and local voting rights for women; others work for

national suffrage. In Washington, DC, they picketed, demonstrated, and builded and maintained

"perpetual watchfires" in which they burned the speeches on democracy that President Wilson

was giving in Europe.

  When the protesters were arrested at the White House in 1917, police had to use personal

cars to carry the many prisoners they arrest. After the women and some of their supporters were

tried and found guilty, the judge got so tired of sentencing them that when he reached twenty-

six, he dismiss all the others.

  The women's organizing and demonstrating finally paid off. On May 21, 1919, the House of

Representatives passed the Nineteenth Amendment, giving women the right to vote, and sended

it to the Senate. On June 4, the Senate approved it and passed it along to the states for ratifi-

cation.

  Women's groups keeped up the pressure on the states during the long, tense ratification

process. When, after more than a year, thirty-five states had ratified the amendment, it all come

down to one man's vote in Tennessee. Who do history remember as the hero of ratification? A

young legislator named Harry Burn, who cast the tie-breaking vote. On August 24, the governor

of Tennessee certified the vote and sent the results to Washington.

  The US secretary of state had tell his staff to wake him as soon as the certificate arrived.

He wanted to avoid a formal signing in the presence of the campaigning women. Nevertheless,

on August 26, 1920, more than seventy years after women had first began to organize for suf-

frage, it was now official: Women in the United States had the right to vote.

**EXERCISE 27-3    Verb forms**    To read about this topic, see section 27 in *Rules for Writers*, Sixth Edition.

---

Edit the following paragraphs for problems with *-s* and *-ed* verb forms. The first revision has been done for you. You should make ten more.

         *have*
Many historians ~~has~~ agreed that the woman suffrage movement in the United States is rooted in the Seneca Falls Convention of 1848. The convention was organize by Elizabeth Cady Stanton and Lucretia Mott, after Mott was denied a seat as a delegate at an antislavery convention in London.

The Seneca Falls Convention is best known for a document produce by Stanton called the Declaration of Sentiments. Stanton's declaration remain one of the most important documents in American women's history. Modeled on the Declaration of Independence (1776), the Declaration of Sentiments list eighteen grievances—but these are grievances of women against their treatment by men and male-dominated society. Stanton's declaration explicitly state that "all men and women are created equal" and that women "demand the equal station to which they are entitled."

A modern reader don't have to read more than a few sentences of each document to see the similarities between the two. In fact, it have been said that the Declaration of Sentiments might have been rejected if its format hadn't seemed so familiar to those who attended the convention. The Declaration of Independence demand that men in America, like men in England, be represented in government. The Declaration of Sentiments argue that women, like men, should be represented in government. The women's document go so far as to suggest that American women should have the right to vote. In 1848, this idea was shocking—so shocking that it would take seventy-two years for the women's vote to become a reality.

## EXERCISE 27-4     Verb forms: Guided review

Correct any nonstandard verb usage in the following paragraphs. The numbers in the margin refer to appropriate rules in section 27 of *Rules for Writers,* Sixth Edition. The first revision has
been done for you.

Today's American woman in a voting booth probably ~~don't~~ *doesn't* know how hard it    27c
was to gain her the right to be there. It took thousands of women nearly a hundred
years to win that freedom for today's voter. Many of those women who worked for
suffrage are no longer knowed, but their names should never be losted to history.    27a, 27a

From the first organized call for woman suffrage in 1848 through the end of the
nineteenth century, feminists such as Elizabeth Cady Stanton, Lucretia Mott, Lucy
Stone, and Susan B. Anthony remained strong voices for women's rights. The next
generation of activists included Harriet Blatch, the youngest daughter of Stanton,
who carry on her mother's work, and Alice Blackwell, the daughter of Lucy Stone,    27d
who continued to edit the *Women's Journal,* which her mother had founded.

In the early 1900s, the women took their cause to Washington. Just before
President Wilson's first inauguration in 1913, activist Inez Milholland, dressed in
white and riding a white horse, leaded eight thousand women in a march through    27a
Washington in support of the suffrage amendment. When she died at age thirty in
1916, a memorial service was held for her under the dome of the US Capitol. She    27e
the first woman so honored.

Alice Paul was a strategist who devoted her life to the suffrage cause, planning
and executing demonstrations and campaigns. Friends worried that she never laid    27b
down to rest but was always working for the cause. Paul's arrest and mistreatment
in prison in 1918 were instrumental in gaining President Wilson's support for the
Nineteenth Amendment. Lucy Burns got involved in woman suffrage in England,
leaving her studies at Oxford to work for the British suffrage movement. When she
come to the United States in 1913, she led others in civil disobedience and was ar-    27a
rested and jailed several times. Carrie Chapman Catt develop the strategy for the fi-    27d
nal years of the battle. Her strategy was called "The Winning Plan" and eventually it
become just that.    27a

Today, most American women takes their voting for granted, unaware of the    27c
thousands of hands that opened that voting booth door for them.

## EXERCISE 27-5    Verb tense and mood: Guided practice

Correct any tense or mood errors in the following paragraphs. The numbers in the margin refer to appropriate rules in section 27 of *Rules for Writers,* Sixth Edition. The first revision has been done for you, and a suggested revision of this exercise appears in the back of the book.

Almost everyone has heard about Aesop's fables, but most people know very little about Aesop himself. Most of what we know about Aesop is a mixture of hearsay and conjecture. We do know that he was a slave in Greece. One theory is that before he came to Greece he *had* lived in Ethiopia for most of his life and that "Aesop" is a much-shortened form of "the Ethiopian."                                                                 27f

Aesop was not a storyteller then, though he would have loved to have spoken well enough to tell a good story. He stuttered so badly that he did not even try to talk. In one story we learn, however, that he could communicate. A neighbor brought a gift of figs to Aesop's master. Greatly pleased, the master planned to enjoy the figs after his bath and directed that they were put in a cool place until he was ready.                27g
While the master was bathing, the overseer and his friends ate the figs. When the master discovered the loss of his figs, the other slaves placed the blame on Aesop. They knew that if Aesop was able to speak, he could defend himself, but they did not                    27g
fear this stammering slave.

The master ordered that Aesop be flogged. Aesop got the master to delay punishment briefly. Aesop drank a glass of warm water, ran his fingers down his throat, and vomited only water. Pointing at the overseer, he made gestures that the overseer and his friends should do as he did. They drank the water, ran their fingers down                     27f
their throats—and vomited figs.

Although Aesop's cleverness saved him from a flogging, it also made an enemy of the overseer. Aesop discovered a basic truth about life: Being right didn't always                  27f
help one to make friends.

## EXERCISE 27-6    Verb tense and mood    To read about this topic, see section 27
in *Rules for Writers*, Sixth Edition.

One sentence in each of the following pairs is correct; the other contains an error in tense or mood. Circle the letters of the correct sentences, and edit the incorrect ones. Example:

     (a.) Aesop was sent to work in the farthest field because he had made an enemy of the overseer.
                *hoped*
     b. Maybe the overseer ~~hope~~ Aesop would run away, or maybe he had forgotten that the field was next
                ^
     to a major road.

1a. One day a caravan that had lost its way came by the field where Aesop was working.

  b. The caravan driver requested that Aesop shows him the route to Cairo.

2a. Aesop, who was unable to speak, wanted to have helped him, so he walked with the caravan until it was on the correct road.

  b. Grateful for Aesop's help and wanting to show his appreciation, the leader offered Aesop a reward.

3a. Aesop silently refused the reward; he had given his help without expecting anything in return.

  b. The caravan leader wanted to leave at once because he lost valuable time on his trip to Cairo.

4a. When the caravan leader said good-bye, he asked the gods to bless Aesop.

  b. As the caravan moved out of sight, Aesop had decided to take a nap.

5a. While Aesop slept, the gods restored his speech, proving that good deeds were sometimes rewarded.

  b. When Aesop awoke and could speak, he rejoiced that the gods help those who befriend strangers.

**EXERCISE 27-7    Verb tense and mood**    To read about this topic, see section 27 in *Rules for Writers*, Sixth Edition.

Some of the italicized verbs in the following sentences are correct; others are in the wrong mood. Mark the correct sentences "OK," and change any incorrect verbs. Example:

> **In ancient Greek culture, an overseer usually tried to sell a troublesome slave; if the slave *was* sold, the overseer's life would be easier.    *OK***

1. When his Greek slave owner ordered that Aesop *be* sold, it was hard to find a buyer for him because he was so ugly.

2. Finally Aesop requested that he *be* allowed to sell himself.

3. Aesop knew that if he *was* not so ugly, many buyers would be glad to get him.

4. If he *was* going to find a buyer, Aesop would need to be clever.

5. One day a caravan that *was* in the slave-trading business stopped at Aesop's master's house.

6. The caravan driver requested that the slave owner *sells* him at least one strong slave.

7. The driver saw that Aesop's muscles *were* strong, but Aesop's hunched back and ugly face discouraged him.

8. Aesop realized that his chances of getting away *were* slim.

9. "If I *was* handsome, I would not be useful as a bogeyman to scare any misbehaving children," he said.

10. If he *were* afraid, the caravan owner did not show it; he laughed at Aesop—and bought him.

## EXERCISE 27-8    Verb tense and mood: Guided review

Correct any errors in verb tense or mood in the following paragraphs. The numbers in the margin refer to appropriate rules in section 27 of *Rules for Writers,* Sixth Edition. The first revision has been done for you. You need to make five more.

Aesop's death illustrated the implied moral of his last fable: When two enemies

fight each other, it ~~was~~ *is* wise to watch for a larger enemy of both. Aesop's death came        *27f*

some years after one of his owners gave him his freedom. His former owner would        *27f*

have liked Aesop to have stayed in the same town, but Aesop became an adviser at        *27f*

the courts of several kings.

One of those kings, Croessus, sent Aesop to Delphi to distribute some gifts. The

people of Delphi demanded that he gives them the gifts at once. Aesop refused, hav-        *27g*

ing discovered that the people of Delphi had lied to Croessus about their activities.

The angry people decided that if Aesop was dead, they could distribute the gifts as        *27g*

they pleased. These people threw Aesop over a cliff to his death, but not before Aesop

had told one more story.

In the story, a frog invites a rat to dinner. To help the rat across the river to the

frog's house, the frog ties one of the rat's legs to one of his own. Midstream, the frog

tries to drown the rat. The rat puts up such a fight that an eagle flying overhead sees

the commotion and promptly eats both of them.

"You will succeed in killing me," said Aesop to the people of Delphi, "but a larger

enemy will kill you as well." After Aesop's death, terrible plagues devastated the city.

People believed that the plagues came because of what they did to Aesop. To this        *27f*

day, the expression "blood of Aesop" refers to an innocent person whose death some-

one has avenged.

## REVIEW OF 19–27: Grammar

Edit the following paragraphs to eliminate grammatical errors. The numbers in the margin refer to appropriate rules in sections 19–27 of *Rules for Writers*, Sixth Edition. First try to find and correct the errors on your own. Then look up the rules if you need to. The first revision has been done for you.

*represent*
The fables of Aesop ~~represents~~ the Western root of fable, but there are two                    *21a*
^
strong Eastern roots of fable also: the Panchatantra and the Jataka tales.

The Panchatantra is a collection of stories designed to teach a first prince and

his brothers how to rule over a kingdom. (Until a tutor taught the first prince with

these stories, him and his brothers would never stay in the schoolroom. The boys            *24a*

listened eagerly to this new tutor who their father had found.) They are usually           *25a, 23a*

longer than Western fables and have people as well as animals for characters. Their

tone sounds differently, too. Aesop's fables make gentle fun of people's foibles,          *26b, 20b*

Panchatantra fables teach lessons in how to achieve and hold power. This difference

is easily recognize in the moral to one of the Panchatantra fables: "Do not strike an           *27d*

enemy of iron with a fist of flesh. Wait until your enemy is stranded at the bottom

of a well. Then throw stones upon him."

The stories that carry the name "Jataka" tells about the Buddha and the ad-                    *21a*

ventures he had when he came to earth in various incarnations. In these stories, the

Buddha appeared as an animal. Or sometimes simply as a "wise old man." Like the           *27f, 19b*

Panchatantra stories, the Jataka tales often depict people's foibles and shortcom-

ings, but the Jataka tales are not satiric. They promote compassion rather than

power. In one story, for example, monkeys try to help their friend the gardener by

watering newly planted trees for him. In doing so, they pull each tree out of the

ground to see how long their roots are. Of course the trees die. The Buddha com-                *22a*

ments, "The ignorant and foolish, even when they desire to do good, often do ill."

Putting all three traditions of fable together, any reader can choose from a rich

combination of small stories that carry large messages.

# EXERCISE 28-1     ESL verb use: Guided practice

Edit the following paragraphs to correct problems with verbs. The numbers in the margin refer to appropriate rules in section 28 of *Rules for Writers,* Sixth Edition. The first revision has been done for you, and a suggested revision of this exercise appears in the back of the book.

    Immigrants have ~~came~~ *come* to the United States from all over the world. Initially,     *28a*

new settlers were mostly European, Irish, or English. By the twentieth century,

many Asians had took the frightening boat trip across the Pacific. Usually the men     *28a*

came first. After they had made enough money for passage, their wives and children

were bring over. All thought that if they worked hard, they will make a good life, as     *28c, 28e*

earlier European immigrants had done. Unable to live comfortably in their home-

lands, a large number of Chinese and Japanese settled in the western part of the

United States.

    These new immigrants worked on the railroads and in the mines. American

businesses recruited Chinese labor because American workers would accept not the     *28d*

wages that were paying. Why did workers decided to come to America anyway?     *28c*

Somehow the idea got started that America was a "golden mountain," where people

could picked up gold nuggets after an easy climb. Once they got here, most immi-     *28b*

grants worked hard because they hoped making enough money to bring relatives to     *28f*

America too.

    Before and during World War II, many Germans who had been persecuted by

Hitler escaped to America. After the war, thousands of "displaced persons" were wel-

come by the United States. Later, refugees from Asia, Africa, Latin America, and the     *28c*

Caribbean wanted being accepted. Franklin D. Roosevelt once said, "All of our     *28f*

people all over the country, except the pure-blooded Indians, are immigrants or de-

scendants of immigrants." If Roosevelt were alive today, he will know that his     *28e*

statement still true.     *28a*

**EXERCISE 28-2**    **Verb forms**    To read about this topic, see section 28a in *Rules for Writers*, Sixth Edition.

Edit the verb in each sentence to match the form indicated in brackets. One sentence is already correct. Mark it "OK." Example:

> *entered*
> **People from many countries ~~enter~~ the United States in the 1980s. [Past]**
> ^

1.  Eighty percent of the immigrants who were allow to come to the United States in the 1980s were Asian or Latin American. [Past]

2.  The number of Asians who were lived in the United States more than doubled between 1970 and 1980. [Past progressive]

3.  People from the Philippines, China, and Korea been regular immigrants to the United States. [Present perfect]

4.  Since 1975, a rush of immigrant refugees been arriving in the United States. [Present perfect progressive]

5.  In less than a seven-year period, 600,000 refugees from Vietnam, Laos, and Cambodia came to the United States. [Past]

## EXERCISE 28-3    Helping verbs, main verbs, and omitted verbs    To read
about this topic, see sections 28a through 28d in *Rules for Writers*, Sixth Edition.

A.  In the following sentences, underline the correct phrase in parentheses. Example:

(Haven't you hear, <u>Haven't you heard</u>) of Eckeo Kounlavong?

1.  Eckeo Kounlavong (was born, had born) in Laos, lived in a refugee camp in Thailand, and
    now lives in Nashville, Tennessee.

2.  Many people (do not knew, do not know) that in Laos, Eckeo was the leader of the Royal
    Laotian Classical Dance Troupe.

3.  Before him, the troupe (had been directed, had been directing) by his father and grand-
    father.

4.  In those days in Laos, the law said that the families of all the dancers (must living, must
    live) in the palace.

5.  They (could not to dance, could not dance) for anyone except the king and his guests.

B.  Edit the following sentences for incorrect use of verbs. Put "OK" next to the one correct sen-
    tence. Example:

                    *changed*
    The dancers' lives were ~~change~~ drastically when the Communists gained power in Laos.
               ^

6.  Eckeo and his mother escaped from Laos to the Nongkhai refugee camp in Thailand.

7.  The troupe resettled in Nashville, Tennessee; they been in Nashville ever since.

8.  Since 1980, Nashville has attract many Laotians.

9.  Nashville has long been knowing as the country music capital of the United States.

10. Now Nashville can claims that it is the capital for country music and for classical Laotian
    music.

Name _____ Section _____ Date _____

**EXERCISE 28-4    Helping verbs and main verbs**    To read about this topic, see section 28 in *Rules for Writers*, Sixth Edition.

Insert appropriate helping verbs in the following sentences. Example:

Immigrants ____*have*____ brought much music to the United States.

1. Most people _____ heard of Seiji Ozawa, the former music director of the Boston Symphony Orchestra.

2. Ozawa _____ born in China and studied music in Japan from a young age.

3. Eileen Farrell, who _____ known internationally as a Metropolitan Opera star, is the daughter of the Irish "Singing O'Farrells."

4. Americans _____ been awed by Chinese cellist Yo-Yo Ma.

5. Chou Wen-chung, a Chinese American composer, _____ awarded a Guggenheim Fellowship.

6. Before his death in 1994, the Chinese American singer Yi-Kwei Sze _____ sung with major orchestras all over the world.

7. The name Myung-Whun Chung _____ not yet be a household word.

8. Many critics were not suprised that he _____ become one of American's outstanding pianists and conductors.

9. Mischa Elman, Jascha Heifetz, and Nathan Milstein, all famous American violinists, _____ born in Russia and immigrated to the United States.

10. Most immigrant musicians _____ not leave their roots behind but used their native culture to enrich the music they have created in the United States.

**EXERCISE 28-5**   **Verb forms**   To read about this topic, see section 28d in *Rules for Writers*, Sixth Edition.

Turn each of the following sentence openings into a complete sentence using the correct main verb form. Choose from these verbs: *give, name, take, buy, offer*. Example:

> **I did not** _____

1. They had been _____

2. He could not _____

3. An award was _____

4. She has already _____

5. They must _____

6. Immigrants have _____

7. Your father has not _____

8. My uncle could _____

9. The house is _____

10. I have been _____

**EXERCISE 28-6**    **Passive verbs**    To read about this topic, see section 28 in *Rules for Writers*, Sixth Edition.

Edit the italicized verb or verb phrase in each of the following sentences to correct the error in the use of the passive voice. (The revised verbs should all be in the passive voice.) Example:

> In the early twentieth century, so many immigrants wanted to enter the United States that a special
>              *built*
> center was ~~build~~ to process them.
>          ^

1.  That center, Ellis Island, *had built* to handle five thousand people a day, but often ten thousand people were processed in one day.

2.  All immigrants *were check* by a doctor, and an immigrant's coat was marked with a code if a problem was suspected.

3.  Everyone knew that if an immigrant *was gave* an "X," the immigrant had practically no chance to enter America; an "X" meant "possible mental problems."

4.  Sometimes families were divided because one child was rejected for some reason; often the child *would sent* back alone.

5.  Although it was the entrance to a new life for many people, "Ellis Island" *was translate* as "Isle of Tears" in many European languages.

**EXERCISE 28-7    Conditional verbs**    To read about this topic, see section 28 in
*Rules for Writers*, Sixth Edition.

Edit the following paragraph to correct problems with conditional verbs. The first revision has
been done for you. You should make five more.

     If my grandfather had immigrated today, instead of eighty years ago, he probably
*would*
~~will~~ have traveled by jet. He came from Croatia to the United States just before the First
^
World War. In those days, when people left their native country, they usually do so forever.
My grandfather missed Croatia, but he liked America very much. He always said that
America was a country where if you work hard, you would be successful. My grandfather,
who will be ninety-five years old if he were alive today, was not as successful as he had
hoped. If he has earned more money, he would have gone back to Croatia to visit. I'm sure
my grandfather will have enjoyed that trip if he had ever had the chance to make it.

## EXERCISE 28-8    Verbs followed by gerunds or infinitives    To read about this
topic, see section 28f in *Rules for Writers*, Sixth Edition.

A.  The gerunds and infinitives are italicized in the following sentences. Only one in each sentence is correct; correct the other one. Example:

Among the many Laotian refugees in Thailand's Nongkhai refugee camp were some members of the
Royal Laotian Classical Dance Troupe. They wanted ~~continuing~~ *to continue* their dancing and discussed *finding* ways that they could stay together.

1.  In the refugee camp in Thailand, the dance troupe began *to think* about *to resettle* together.

2.  They enjoyed *to work* together on their music and liked *to perform* for others.

3.  Someone suggested *discussing* the idea with resettlement officials who might let them *staying* together.

4.  The Laotians wanted *living* together; they asked the officials *to move* the seventy dancers and their families—260 people—to one place.

5.  They did not expect anyone *agreeing* to their proposal; nevertheless, they enjoyed *thinking* about it.

B.  Correct the use of gerunds and infinitives in the following sentences. Put "OK" next to the one correct sentence. Example:

The United States allowed the Laotian dancers ~~coming~~ *to come* to America together.

6.  The officials let them to bring all their equipment and costumes for performing in their new country.

7.  Refugee officials needed to handle thousands of pieces of paper for the dancers before they finished to process them.

8.  To avoid splitting up the troupe, officials asked resettlement agencies in America finding sponsors for all of the dancers and their families in one community.

9.  People in Nashville, Tennessee, offered to let the troupe settle there.

10. The Laotians wanted thanking the people of Nashville by giving a concert for the city.

## EXERCISE 28-9    ESL verb use: Guided review

Edit the following paragraphs to correct errors in the use of verbs. The numbers in the margin refer to appropriate rules in section 28 of *Rules for Writers*, Sixth Edition. The first sentence has been revised for you.

                                         *adapted*
    Although most refugee immigrants have ~~adapt~~ well to life in America, some                28a
                                              ^

have not. Many have great difficulty learning English and accepting the customs of

this land they have came to. Other newcomers find that they miss their former                28a

homes more than they thought they would. They believe that they would have been

much happier if they have stayed in their native countries. Among the Laotians, the          28e

saddest stories indicate that homesickness can even cause death. Would you believe

that homesickness can be so powerful? Young Laotian men with no apparent health

problems have died suddenly in their sleep. Doctors can to give no reason for these           28b

deaths, but Laotians believe that the young men wanted going home too much. They             28f

say that their bodies died so that their spirits could enjoy to go home again.                28f

    Immigrants from Mexico, Cuba, and Puerto Rico have had problems, too. Many

Mexican immigrants been forcibly repatriated because the American government                  28c

considered them "illegal" immigrants. Most Cuban immigrants in the 1960s ex-

pected their stay in America to be temporary, so they did no become US citizens.              28d

Because Puerto Ricans are US citizens, they are not really "immigrants." They are            28a

look for a better life, although they do not always find it. So many Puerto Ricans

have returned to their homeland that they have been give a special name,                      28c

"Neoricans."

    Most immigrants, however, have adjust to the new country, changing them-            28a

selves—and it.

## EXERCISE 29-1   Articles: Guided practice

Edit the following paragraphs to correct the use of articles. The numbers in the margin refer to appropriate rules in section 29 of *Rules for Writers*, Sixth Edition. The first revision has been done for you, and a suggested revision of this exercise appears in the back of the book.

People all over the world have stories that are part of their culture. Many cul-

tures have *a* creation story that explains how the world came to be. Sometimes story      *29d, 29c*

tells how a single piece of the world got its characteristics. It is not surprising that

these stories exist; what is surprising is how similar the stories are. Consider

Cinderella story, for example. Cinderella has different names in different places,      *29c*

and details of her adventure are not the same; but the basic story echoes around a      *29c*

world.

In the Egypt, she is called Rhodopis (the word means "rosy cheeked"). Rhodopis      *29g*

is a Greek slave in a Egyptian home. She does not have eyes or an hair like anyone      *29a, 29e*

else in the home. Her green eyes look quite different from eyes of the other girls.      *29c*

Their dark, straight hair almost never gets tangled; her yellow, curly hair blows into

tangled mass around her face. her light-skinned face turns red and burns when she      *29d*

is in sun too long. When someone calls her "Rosy Rhodopis," she blushes, and her      *29c*

cheeks become rosier.

Unable to make the friends with the other girls, Rhodopis turns to the animals      *29f*

in the nearby woods and streams.

**EXERCISE 29-2**   **Articles**   To read about this topic, see section 29 in *Rules for Writers*, Sixth Edition.

Some of the following sentences have errors in the use of articles. Mark the correct sentences "OK," and correct the others. Example:

Rhodopis charmed the animals: birds, monkeys, and even ~~an~~ $\overset{a}{\wedge}$ hippopotamus would do what she asked.

1. The animals loved to watch her dance; her tiny feet seemed never to touch path.

2. One night when her owner saw her dancing, he was enchanted and decided that such feet deserved special shoes.

3. Rhodopis's shoes had the leather soles, but the toes had a gold on them.

4. When Rhodopis danced, shoes sparkled; they seemed alive.

5. Jealous, the servant girls gave her the more chores; by nighttime, Rhodopis was almost too tired for a single dance.

6. Pharaoh, the ruler of Egypt, sent out a invitation for all his subjects to appear at a court festival.

7. Everyone wanted to go to festival; Rhodopis looked forward to dancing there.

8. The other girls gave her extra chores so that she would not be able to get away: washing the clothes, grinding the grain, and planting the garden.

9. While Rhodopis was doing a laundry, a hippopotamus splashed into the water.

10. The splash muddied Rhodopis's shoes; she cleaned the shoes and set them high on the riverbank to keep them safe.

**EXERCISE 29-3**    **Articles**    To read about this topic, see section 29 in *Rules for Writers*, Sixth Edition.

Some of the following sentences has one missing or misused article. Mark the correct sentences "OK," and correct the others. Example:

                                                                                  *a*
Almost as soon as Rhodopis put her slippers on the bank, huge shadow fell over the land.
                                                                                  ^

1. Rhodopis looked up and saw an huge falcon flying overhead.

2. Rhodopis bowed her head, recognizing the falcon as a symbol of great god Horus.

3. She greeted the bird politely; but when bird flew away, he took one of her slippers with him.

4. Tearful, Rhodopis tucked the other slipper into her tunic and resumed a work.

5. She tried to imagine dancing on one foot; idea made her laugh.

6. The bird flew to Memphis, went to the festival, and found the Pharaoh, Amasis.

7. Amasis sat on his throne, immobilized by a boredom; then the bird dropped the shoe into his lap.

8. Amasis recognized Horus in the falcon and decided that the shoe was a sign to tell him whom he should marry.

9. Amasis got into his chariot to look all through Egypt for owner of the shoe, who he knew would be his bride.

10. All of people went home from the festival, including the servant girls who had left Rhodopis at home.

## EXERCISE 29-4    Articles: Guided review

Edit the following paragraphs to correct the use of articles. The numbers in the margin refer to appropriate rules in section 29 of *Rules for Writers*, Sixth Edition. The first revision has been done for you.

Pharaoh Amasis traveled all over ~~the~~ Egypt searching for his bride-to-be. The          *29g*

search took the very long time. Everywhere, beautiful women came to put their feet          *29d*

into a rose-gold slipper he carried with him. Not one of them could fit her foot into          *29c*

so small a shoe.

When Amasis had not found the owner of the shoe in his own land, he decided

to look along Nile River. His boats were brightly decorated, and musicians made an          *29g, 29a*

loud noise of trumpets and gongs as they traveled. The noise attracted many people

to river, but Rhodopis was so frightened that she ran to hide in a weed patch. Amasis          *29c*

stopped his boat so that the people along the shore could reach him and pay an at-          *29e*

tention to his words.

When Amasis held out the slipper, all of the servant girls made effort to wear it;          *29d*

it fit no one. Then Amasis saw Rhodopis in weeds and ordered her to try also. The          *29c*

shoe fit, and Rhodopis pulled its mate out of her tunic.

Wearing both slippers, Rhodopis joined Amasis on a boat. Rhodopis was on her          *29c*

way to an happy life as the new queen of Egypt.          *29a*

## EXERCISE 30/31-1    Sentence structure, prepositions, and idiomatic expressions: Guided practice

Edit the following paragraphs to correct any misuses of subjects, repetitions, adverbs, adjectives, participles, and prepositions. The numbers in the margin refer to appropriate rules in sections 30 and 31 of *Rules for Writers*, Sixth Edition. The first revision has been done for you, and a suggested revision of this exercise appears in the back of the book.

A descendant of one of the earliest immigrants ~~at~~ *to* North America played a pivotal role in helping later Americans explore their country. Were tribes of American Indians living all over what is now the United States. Each tribe had its own language and customs. Some tribes raided others and took prisoners who then became the raiding tribes' slaves. That is what happened to a young Shoshone girl now known as Sacagawea. | 31a<br>30b

This girl, like many young girls, she had a nickname, "He-toe." "He-toe" was the sound a local bird made, and the girl's movements were so swift that friends thought she resembled that bird. When a raiding party of Hidatsas captured easily this young girl, they named her Sacagawea—"bird woman." Sacagawea was about twelve years old. The frightening young girl did not try to escape but accepted her role and worked for her captors. At a few months, she had acquired a reputation for good sense and good work. | 30c<br>30f<br>30g<br>31a

The tribe married Sacagawea to a white man, Toussaint Charbonneau; she was his second wife. Soon pregnant, this typical Indian wife she did the chores and left all decisions to her husband; but inwardly, she longed to explore new places and meet new people. She may have been controlling by her husband, but she never missed a chance to learn whatever she could. | 30c<br>30g

When white men appeared, many Indians were curious. Sacagawea had never seen a man with yellow hair—or red hair. Nor had she ever seen a black man. All these men were trying to get to the "Big Water" far to the west. They would have to cross mountains that they had not even seen them yet. They needed horses and guides that the Shoshones could supply and an interpreter who could speak the Shoshone language. Imagine their surprise when this interpreter, whom they had hoped to find him, turned out to be a woman—a Shoshone young attractive woman. | 30d<br>30d, 30h

**EXERCISE 30/31-2    Omissions and needless repetitions**    To read about this topic, see sections 30b and 30c in *Rules for Writers,* Sixth Edition.

---

In the following sentences, add needed subjects or expletives and delete any repeated subjects, objects, or adverbs. Mark the two correct sentences "OK." Example:

> The white men who came ashore ~~they~~ had been sent by the Great White Father in Washington to blaze a trail to the Big Water.

1.  The two leaders among the white men they were Meriwether Lewis and William Clark.

2.  Clark's red beard and hair puzzled Sacagawea; was hard to believe that those red hairs were real.

3.  Sacagawea also watched in amazement as York, the black man, he washed his hands and face and none of his color came off.

4.  The men quickly began building the shelters that they were going to live in them.

5.  Was a lot of noise as they felled trees and fitted the logs together to build cabins.

6.  The white men hired Charbonneau as an interpreter (he spoke both Hidatsa and French) and told him to bring Sacagawea along too.

7.  Sacagawea could hardly believe that she would see her own people again in the place where she had lived there before.

8.  Charbonneau and Sacagawea, who was now near the end of her pregnancy, were given a cabin to live in that winter.

9.  Sacagawea's friends came often to the house that she was staying in it, usually asking for medical help while they were there.

10. Sacagawea, who learned how to cook for the white men, she tried especially to please Captain Clark, who gave her an English name, Janie.

## EXERCISE 30/31-3    Present and past participles    To read about this topic, see
section 30g in *Rules for Writers*, Sixth Edition.

Circle the letter of the sentence that answers the question. Example:

> **In which sentence were the men eager to get started?**
>
> **a. By April, the snows were melting and the men in the camp were exciting to begin moving on.**
>
> **(b.) By April, the snows were melting and the men in the camp were excited to begin moving on.**

1. In which sentence were the men happy?

    a. Sacagawea always found the men pleasing.

    b. Sacagawea always found the men pleased.

2. In which sentence was Sacagawea eager to get to the mountains?

    a. As they neared the mountains, where the Shoshone lived, Sacagawea grew more and more excited.

    b. As they neared the mountains, where the Shoshone lived, Sacagawea grew more and more exciting.

3. In which sentence did Clark enjoy watching Sacagawea?

    a. Watching Sacagawea bargain for horses, Clark was fascinating.

    b. Watching Sacagawea bargain for horses, Clark was fascinated.

4. In which sentence were the travelers unhappy?

    a. For the four months they stayed on the West Coast, the travelers had only twelve days without rain; all of them found this weather depressed.

    b. For the four months they stayed on the West Coast, the travelers had only twelve days without rain; all of them found this weather depressing.

5. In which sentence did the decision make everyone fearful?

    a. On the way home, Lewis and Clark made a frightened decision to divide the crew and send the men along different trails.

    b. On the way home, Lewis and Clark made a frightening decision to divide the crew and send the men along different trails.

**EXERCISE 30/31-4    Placement of adjectives**    To read about this topic, see section 30h in *Rules for Writers*, Sixth Edition.

Insert the adjectives in their correct positions in the following sentences. Do not add commas. Example:

old, experienced

*Experienced* *old* women came to help Sacagawea when it was time for her baby to be born.

1. log, warm

   Sacagawea was glad that she was living in a _____ _____ cabin when birthing time came.

2. hard, labor

   The baby did not come easily. Neither the old women's skill nor Captain Clark's medicines did much to ease Sacagawea's _____ _____ pains.

3. the, old, bell-shaped

   Finally, one of the men said that swallowing some rattles (_____ _____ _____ scales on a rattlesnake's tail) often brought a quick and easy birth.

4. dark, strange, this

   Captain Clark had collected some rattles; he crushed two of them and added some water. One of the old women gave _____ _____ _____ potion to Sacagawea.

5. male, a, healthy

   Ten minutes later, Jean Baptiste Charbonneau arrived—_____ _____ _____ child who would be affectionately called "Pomp," the Shoshone word for "firstborn."

## EXERCISE 30/31-5    Sentence structure, prepositions, and idiomatic expressions: Guided review

Edit the following paragraphs to correct any misuses of subjects, expletives, adjectives, adverbs, participles, and prepositions. Do not change correct sentences. The numbers in the margin refer to appropriate rules in sections 30 and 31 of *Rules for Writers*, Sixth Edition. The first revision has been done for you.

By the time Lewis and Clark ~~found~~ *finally* the Pacific Ocean and made their way                30f
home again, Sacagawea not only had gotten her wish to travel but also had become
a favorite of all the crew. Had served as interpreter, guide, cook, nurse, and mother                30b
for everyone who needed her. She and Pomp seemed like family to Clark and his
men.

When Captain Clark left, he offered to take Pomp (now almost two) to St. Louis
and educate him. Sacagawea said, "Not now," but later the whole family moved in                     31a
St. Louis. No one is sure what happened next. Most historians agree that after a few
months Charbonneau left gladly St. Louis "with his wife" and spent time at a new                     30f
fort, Fort Manuel. There his wife she sickened and died of a fever in 1812. Since                     30c
Charbonneau had several Shoshone wives, cannot be sure that this wife was                             30b
Sacagawea. Historical records show that Clark became the legal guardian for Pomp
and his baby sister the year that Charbonneau's wife died.

Pomp stayed with Captain Clark. At nineteen, he met a German rich prince who                         30h
was touring America and went to Europe with him for six years. Later this moun-
tain man, whose mother had trekked with him halfway across the continent before
he could walk, he returned to mountain life for good, working as a trader, a hunter,                  30c
and an interpreter.

The Shoshone oral tradition says that Sacagawea quarreled with Charbonneau
and left him, stayed for a while with the Comanches, met up with her son and a
nephew, and ended up at the Wind River Reservation in Wyoming, where she died
on April 4, 1884, almost one hundred years old. The Wyoming branch of the
Daughters of the American Revolution were convincing that the oral tradition was                      30g
true and erected a memorial stone there.

No other American woman has had so many memorials dedicated to her. Among them are historical markers, lakes, a river, a mountain peak, and a park. On 1999, the United States even honored her on its new dollar—a gold-colored coin. Just below the word *Liberty* on that coin is a likeness of Sacagawea with her infant son. Now travel-loving Sacagawea can go wherever that dollar goes there.

31a

30d

## REVIEW OF 28–31: ESL challenges

This paragraph has eleven errors. The numbers in the margin refer to appropriate rules in sections 28–31 of *Rules for Writers*, Sixth Edition. The first revision has been done for you. Find and correct ten more errors.

      Immigrants have ~~gave~~ <sup>given</sup> the United States their languages, their foods, and their     *28a*

customs. Native Americans gave the United States the names for half of its states.

*Texas* is an Indian old word for "friends," and *Idaho* means "good morning." Spanish     *30h*

immigrants gave the United States the longest name for any of its cities. In Spanish,

is *El Pueblo de Nuestra Señora la Reina de los Angeles de Porciúncula*—Los     *30b*

Angeles. American cuisine now includes foods of many other traditions, from

Chinese sweet-and-sour pork to Greek baklava. American children who enjoy to eat     *28f*

pizza or spaghetti or tacos think they are eating American food. Since the Germans

brought the Christmas tree to America, every immigrant group that celebrates

Christmas it has added something to American Christmas customs. Fiestas and ser-     *30c*

enades are common in the United States, and even New England children often want

breaking a piñata on their birthday parties. Every summer in Washington, DC,     *28f, 31a*

Americans celebrate the diversity of their culture with an excited folk festival.     *30g*

Groups from many different cultures in America bring an equipment to produce     *29f*

their own foods and festivities on the national Mall, where many other Americans

can enjoy them. A alien visitor from Mars would not be able to tell which songs and     *29a*

stories are "American," for the food, festivals, dances, music, and folktales of immi-

grant groups have became part of America's own culture.     *28a*

## EXERCISE 32/33-1    The comma and unnecessary commas: Guided practice

Edit the following essay by adding commas where they are needed and removing unnecessary commas. The numbers in the margin refer to appropriate rules in sections 32 and 33 of *Rules for Writers*, Sixth Edition. The first revision has been done for you, and answers to this exercise appear in the back of the book.

If a boy wanted to join the football team at Carlisle Indian School, he had to go          32b
through a difficult test. Any boy who wanted to be on the team had to stand at one
of the goal lines; all the first-string players stood around the field. When the ball was
punted to the new boy, he had to catch it and try to get all the way to the other end
zone with it. The team members tried to stop him before he could get very far. Only
a few players had ever gotten as far as the fifty-yard line so "Pop" Warner, coach at          32a
the Carlisle Indian School considered it a good test.          32e

One day a quiet Indian boy surprised Pop. The boy caught the ball, started running, wheeled away from the first players who tried to stop him, shook off the others and ran the ball all the way to the opposite goal line. Convinced that the player's          32c
success was an accident, the coach ordered him to run the play again. Brusquely,
the coach spoke to the players, and reminded them that this workout was supposed          33a
to be tackling practice. Jim, the nineteen-year-old six-footer, simply said "Nobody          32h
tackles Jim." Then he ran the ball to the goal line a second time.

Well, almost no one tackled Jim Thorpe successfully for many years. Life itself
got him down and made him fumble more often than his football opponents did, but,          33h
he was usually able to recover and go on. The first blow was the death of his twin
brother while the two boys were still in grade school. This tragedy was followed by
others; by the time Jim was twenty-five, he had lost his brother, his mother, and his
father to death. They left him a Native American heritage: His father was half Irish
and half Native American and his mother was the granddaughter of a famous,          32a, 33d
Indian warrior named Chief Black Hawk.

Fortunately or unfortunately, along with his Native American heritage came great pride and stoicism. That pride kept him silent when the greatest blow of all came: He was forced to return the Olympic medals he had won in 1912 because he was declared to be not an amateur. He dealt stoically with his personal tragedies. When infantile paralysis struck his son Jim Thorpe disappeared for a few days to deal with the tragedy alone. His stoicism also saw him through a demotion to the minor leagues and sad years of unemployment and poverty before his death.

*32b*

Even death's tackle may not have been totally successful: After Jim Thorpe's death his Olympic medals were returned, and a town was named after him.

*32b*

**EXERCISE 32/33-2**     **The comma**     To read about this topic, see sections 32 and 33 in *Rules for Writers*, Sixth Edition.

A. Insert commas where they are needed with coordinating conjunctions in the following sentences. If a sentence is correct, mark it "OK." Example:

**Coach Warner was impressed with the new player's skill, and he looked for a chance to try him in an actual game.**

1. Jim passed Coach Warner's test but he did not get to play right away.

2. Then in one game a player was injured and Coach Warner sent Jim in.

3. At first, no one but Jim and the coach believed that Jim could play well enough.

4. He lost five yards the first time he got the ball but the next time he ran sixty-five yards for a touchdown.

5. His sports career began with that game and included major honors in track, lacrosse, baseball, and football.

B. Insert commas when they are needed after an introductory element, in a series, and with coordinate adjectives. If a sentence is correct, mark it "OK." Example:

**After trying to tackle Thorpe only once, Jim's most famous opponent never played football again.**

6. In a game against Army, Carlisle's Thorpe had the ball.

7. One Army player tried to tackle Jim, failed, injured his knee in the process and had to be helped from the field.

8. That strong confident player said in later years, "Thorpe gained ground; he *always* gained ground."

9. Although the injured player was never able to play football again he became famous in other ways.

10. He became supreme commander of the Allied armies in Europe in World War II and thirty-fourth president of the United States—Dwight D. Eisenhower.

**EXERCISE 32/33-3    The comma**    To read about this topic, see sections 32 and 33 in *Rules for Writers*, Sixth Edition.

A. Add commas where needed around nonrestrictive elements. If a sentence is correct, mark it "OK." Example:

Jim Thorpe's Olympic medals, which he won in 1912 but had to forfeit, were for the pentathlon and the decathlon. [Thorpe won Olympic medals only in 1912.]

1. The Carlisle students who needed summer jobs often played baseball for Carolina teams. [Not all Carlisle students needed summer jobs.]

2. The players who were willing to lie used false names when they played for little-known teams; Jim did not. [Only some of the players were willing to lie.]

3. Those who had received money for playing their sport were disqualified because they were no longer "amateurs." [Only some received money.]

4. The five-sport event which is called the pentathlon is difficult. [There is only one five-sport event.]

5. The decathlon which is a ten-sport event is considered the most difficult of all Olympic events. [There is only one ten-sport event.]

B. Add commas as necessary in the following sentences. Example:

In Stockholm, Sweden's King Gustav presented the 1912 Olympic winners with their gold medals; in addition, he spoke briefly to some of them.

6. As King Gustav presented Jim Thorpe's 1912 Olympic medal, he said to Jim "Sir you are the greatest athlete in the world."

7. In January 1913 however a newspaper reported that Jim had been paid for playing for the Carolina baseball teams.

8. When the Amateur Athletic Union (AAU) asked Jim said he had been paid.

9. Stating that he had not known he was doing wrong, Jim insisted that he had acted no worse than athletes who used false names.

10. Jim having presented his case, the AAU made its ruling; specifically it ruled that Jim had not been an amateur at the time of the Olympics.

**EXERCISE 32/33-4**    **The comma**    To read about this topic, see sections 32 and 33 in *Rules for Writers*, Sixth Edition.

---

Edit the following paragraphs to correct the use of commas. The first revision has been done for you. You should add ten more commas.

When the Amateur Athletic Union ruled that 1912 Olympic winner Jim Thorpe had not been an amateur at the time he won his medals, several consequences followed. Once the ruling was formally stated, Jim Thorpe's name was erased from the Olympic records. In addition he had to return his medals. Friends wanted him to fight the AAU ruling but he was too proud to do so.

During the next sixteen years that Jim played football was quite different from what it is today. Players then had no league, no formal schedule, no required helmets and often no salaries. Then representatives of eight concerned teams met to form a league. The organization they formed which was called the American Professional Football Association later became the National Football League; Jim Thorpe was its first president.

Jim's playing declined with the years until on November 30, 1929 an Associated Press story described him as "a mere shadow of his former self." No longer able to play sports Thorpe had to dig ditches in the Depression years. When the 1932 Olympics were held in Los Angeles California he could not afford to buy a ticket.

**EXERCISE 32/33-5    Unnecessary commas**    To read about this topic, see sections 32 and 33 in *Rules for Writers*, Sixth Edition.

Each of the following sentences has one unnecessary comma. Delete the comma that is not needed. Example:

> **Along with other bad news about Thorpe, newspaper stories reported/that he drank too much and that drinking caused his second marriage to go wrong.**

1.  After Jim Thorpe's death, his friends still worked to have his medals restored, and to get his name back on the list of Olympic winners.

2.  Knowing that they would not be happy, until the AAU and the Olympic committees changed their minds, his friends made repeated appeals.

3.  The AAU acted first, reversing itself some years later, (in 1973) by saying that Thorpe's titles should be restored.

4.  The American Olympic Committee agreed two years later, but, it was not until 1982 that the International Olympic Committee voted to restore Jim's titles.

5.  New, Olympic medals were presented to Thorpe's children in a 1983 ceremony in Los Angeles, California.

6.  However, the International Olympic Committee, did not erase the names of the second-place finishers.

7.  Even though Thorpe had beaten the other "winners," his friends had to accept the fact, that Jim would be listed only as a cochampion.

8.  In the hearts of Jim's supporters remains the honest, firm conviction, that Jim should be listed as the sole winner.

9.  They thought that the International Olympic Committee's reversing its position, restoring the titles, and awarding Thorpe's medals to his children, were not enough.

10. It is not likely that there will be any further action, such as, erasing the other winners' names.

**EXERCISE 32/33-6    Unnecessary commas**    To read about this topic, see sections 32 and 33 in *Rules for Writers,* Sixth Edition.

One sentence in each of the following pairs is correctly punctuated. Circle the letter of the correct sentence and edit the incorrect sentence. Example:

(a.) Jim Thorpe was a greater athlete than any other athlete of his time.

b. In 1950, an Associated Press poll of hundreds of sportswriters indicated that Thorpe was better/
than any other athlete from 1900 to 1950.

1a. According to many experts, (sportswriters, coaches, and the like), Thorpe would always be considered the best athlete of his era.

b. Others predicted that modern knowledge of various aspects of training (nutrition, drugs, and the like) would produce even greater players by then.

2a. People said, that Thorpe's confidence in himself was so great that he often skipped practice at the Olympics, and they told the "broad jump story" to illustrate his confidence.

b. Observers said that he measured the broad jump distance with his eye, decided he could jump it, and lay down in a hammock for a nap, not even bothering to take a practice run at it.

3a. In his 289 games in baseball's major leagues, the only statistic that suggested trouble was his batting average of .252.

b. It seems that the only thing that really bothered Jim, was hitting curveballs.

4a. He had a peculiar style of running, that left his football tacklers flat on the ground.

b. He would twist his hips away from the player who was after him.

5a. He would wait until that player's head was at the exact, dangerous, height.

b. Then he would swing his hips with full, direct force right into the player's head.

## EXERCISE 32/33-7    The comma and unnecessary commas: Guided review

Edit the following paragraphs by adding commas where they are needed and removing commas where they are not needed. The numbers in the margin refer to appropriate rules in sections 32 and 33 of *Rules for Writers,* Sixth Edition. The first revision has been done for you.

Quarrels about one of America's greatest athletes, Jim Thorpe, continue. Even though the decision about his Olympic standing has been made, other quarrels about him remain. — 32b

After Jim Thorpe died his wife had to choose a burial place. Everyone assumed he would be buried in his home state of Oklahoma, but, his wife made other arrangements. Some people from Mauch Chunk, Pennsylvania, made her an offer. They said, that they wanted Jim buried in their town. Having his body there would make more tourists want to come to their small, Pennsylvania town. They talked of a burial place, a Jim Thorpe Museum and a hospital in his memory. They also offered to change the name of the town from Mauch Chunk to Jim Thorpe. — 32b — 33h — 33h — 33d — 32c

Mrs. Thorpe, who wanted a memorial for Jim, agreed to these proposals, and gave Jim's body to the town. It is probable that at the core of her decision was the desire for Jim Thorpe to be remembered. After some negotiation, the agreement was concluded and the town is now on the map as "Jim Thorpe." — 33a — 32a

Jim's wife, not his children, made the agreement. His children, seven sons and daughters, wanted his body buried in Oklahoma. They wanted the body to be given a traditional Indian burial. They wanted the town to give back their father's body. Jack Thorpe, one of the sons, said to a *Sports Illustrated* writer in 1982 "Dad's spirit is still roaming." In Jim Thorpe's family pride is still part of the Thorpe heritage. The family has not given up the struggle. Other people have also asked the townspeople to change their minds. — 32h — 32b

Jim Thorpe lived a tough, honest, gifted, and controversial, life. Even if his records are someday broken, he will remain a legend of the American sports world. — 33c

## EXERCISE 34-1    The semicolon: Guided practice

Edit the following paragraphs to correct problems with the use of semicolons. The numbers in the margin refer to appropriate rules in section 34 of *Rules for Writers*, Sixth Edition. The first revision has been done for you, and answers to this exercise appear in the back of the book.

When Cheryl Toussaint came in second in a race she had never planned to run/, she started on a road that led to the Olympics and a world record.        *34d*

Cheryl began running almost by accident one day when she went to watch a city-sponsored track meet in Brooklyn, New York. During the preliminaries, the officials announced an "open" race, it was one that anyone could enter. Cheryl wanted        *34a* to enter; but she was dressed in a skirt and sandals. Four things made her run; one        *34d, 34d* friend traded shoes with her, another let her borrow jeans, several called her "chicken" if she didn't run, and one girl dared her to run. Coming in second in that race led this teenager to many places, including Munich, Germany, Toronto,        *34c* Canada, and Montreal, Canada.

There were, however, many races to run and lessons to learn. Cheryl joined the all-female Atoms Track Club, and she began training under Coach Fred Thompson. Like most coaches, Fred had his own way of testing newcomers. He watched a new runner carefully, however, he gave her no special attention. Instead, he just gave her        *34b* orders one after another. He would tell Cheryl to run laps, go through exercises, and do practice starts, at the same time he would never comment on how she performed.        *34a* If the newcomer endured the hard, time-consuming workouts without encouragement or praise; Thompson was sure that she was ready for real coaching.        *34d*

Cheryl quit after two months, for six more months she stayed out. During that        *34a* time she thought about her attitude toward work, her poor record at school, her pleasure in running, and her lack of goals. When she returned; Thompson welcomed        *34d* her back. Coach Thompson knew how special Cheryl was, he not only convinced her        *34a* she was college material but pushed her to achieve the highest goal of the amateur athlete—the Olympics.

## EXERCISE 34-2    The semicolon    To read about this topic, see section 34 in *Rules for Writers*, Sixth Edition.

Add semicolons in the five word groups that need them; mark the other word groups "OK." Example:

> Cheryl Toussaint's first run was an indication of her character and determination ; no one could find
>
> fault with her effort.

1. Cheryl's first run—at a cross-country meet on Long Island—would certainly have impressed any coach every person watching was astounded by her perseverance.

2. Coach Thompson had warned her not to start too fast but to stay with the pack. "Just try to finish," he said.

3. Too excited to follow his directions, Cheryl took off at top speed at the starting gun, moreover, she did not slow down even after she was a hundred yards in front of everyone else.

4. Cheryl kept that distance for most of the run, she did not allow herself any slack.

5. Then, with only a hundred yards to go, Cheryl gave out, she collapsed and fell down.

6. Immediately, she got to her knees and started crawling. She crawled toward the finish line, not to the grassy area where runners who left the race were supposed to go.

7. She got up, staggered a little farther, and fell again. Once more she started crawling.

8. Not able to get to her feet, Cheryl continued to crawl, after all, she was nearly to the finish line.

9. She had almost reached the line when another runner passed her and won.

10. "I knew at that moment," said her coach, "that this girl was going to be something special." Her coach was right.

**EXERCISE 34-3**    **The semicolon**    To read about this topic, see section 34 in *Rules for Writers*, Sixth Edition.

Each of the following sentences has two semicolons but should have only one. Delete the incorrect one and replace it with other punctuation if necessary. Example:

> No one else had ever seen anything special in Cheryl/, who had never shown any ambition; her teachers had labeled her a "slow learner" long before she got to high school.

1. Cheryl had to beg her teachers to allow her to take college preparatory courses; they were sure she would fail; no matter how hard she tried.

2. Coach Thompson did many things for Cheryl; including coaching track, prodding her about schoolwork, encouraging good eating habits, and insisting that she think about college; most important of all, he gave her faith in herself.

3. All of the runners knew that if they made qualifying times; Coach Thompson would see to it that they were entered in the national meets; however, they also knew that if they did not qualify, they were off the team.

4. Cheryl soon discovered that she had to schedule her time; or she would fail at school or at track or at both; thinking about Coach Thompson, she began to care.

5. By the time Cheryl graduated from high school, she was an A student; this "slow learner" received an academic scholarship to New York University; although she had thought only an athletic one was possible.

## EXERCISE 34-4    The semicolon: Guided review

Edit the following paragraphs to correct problems with use of semicolons. The numbers in the margin refer to appropriate rules in section 34 of *Rules for Writers*, Sixth Edition. The first revision has been done for you.

Every runner dreams of winning both individual and relay medals at the Olympics/; in 1972, Cheryl Toussaint was no exception. When she did not make the individual finals; she pinned her hopes on the relay race. Her teammates on the American team were ready: Mabel Ferguson, Madeline Jackson, and Kathy Hammond. The relay was Cheryl's last chance to win a medal, unfortunately, it seemed that everything was against her.    *34a*    *34d*    *34b*

Cheryl began the third leg of the qualifying heat with runners ahead of her. Then a runner in front of her fell. As Cheryl dashed around her, another runner stepped on the heel of Cheryl's left shoe, so Cheryl was running with her shoe half on and half off. She needed to stop and pull the shoe on, but she knew two things: She would lose valuable time, and this was her team's last chance to qualify for the finals. She kept running, very soon the shoe flew up in the air. Cheryl wondered whether the shoe would hit anyone, whether TV viewers could see her bare foot, and whether people in the stands had noticed. But she ran on, passing the other runners. Her team qualified for the finals that day, and in the finals, Cheryl and her teammates won silver medals.    *34a*

Cheryl remembered her very first run, at which she hadn't even known how to start, her first "real" race, at which she'd crawled to the finish line, and her most recent one, at which she'd failed to qualify for the 800-meter run. She could laugh about all those memories now, for she and her teammates were Olympic winners.    *34c*

Back home, Cheryl kept to her plans: graduating from college (with a B+ average), getting a job in the Federal Reserve Bank's management training program, and starting to train for the next Olympics. She knew that nothing would ever mean as much to her again as track, the Atoms, and Coach Thompson had meant her success was also theirs.    *34a*

## EXERCISE 35-1    The colon: Guided practice

In the following paragraph, insert colons where they are needed and eliminate any improperly used colons. The numbers in the margin refer to appropriate rules in section 35 of *Rules for Writers*, Sixth Edition. The first revision has been done for you, and answers to this exercise appear in the back of the book.

In 1951, Althea Gibson broke the color barrier in women's tennis and became admired all over the world. No one who knew her as a teenager would have predicted her success. By the time Althea Gibson reached her teens, her record showed three indications of trouble: running away from home, dropping out of school, and losing     *35a*

the one job she had been able to find. To survive in her neighborhood, Althea depended on: a small welfare allowance, occasional handouts, and plain old luck. She     *35d*

listed her skills as the following, good bowler, great two-on-two basketball player,     *35a*

and fast paddleball player. Even after she began playing tennis and moving in upper-class Harlem society, she resented the efforts of the society ladies to improve her. They busied themselves with tasks such as: correcting her manners and re-     *35d*

stricting her behavior. Looking back, she later summed up her attitude she said she     *35b*

wasn't ready to study about "how to be a fine lady." At eighteen, she finally got: a     *35d*

waitress job, a congenial roommate, and a good friend.

**EXERCISE 35-2**     **The colon**     To read about this topic, see section 35 in *Rules for Writers*, Sixth Edition.

---

In the following sentences, insert colons where they can be effectively used. Example:

In 1957, Althea Gibson won the women's title at the most prestigious tennis tournament in the world: Wimbledon.

1.  Althea Gibson broke the color barrier in women's tennis she was the first black female player to compete in national championships.

2.  Two tennis-playing doctors opened their homes to her so she could finish high school and go to college Dr. Hubert A. Eaton of Wilmington, North Carolina, and Dr. Robert W. Johnson of Lynchburg, Virginia.

3.  Her life in a southern high school was not pleasant; if she had written a book about it, she could have titled it *Misfit, A Yankee Woman in a Southern School.*

4.  Besides tennis, Althea's other love was music the drums, the chorus, and especially the saxophone.

5.  Her friend Sugar Ray Robinson advised her firmly to go to college "No matter what you want to do, tennis or music or what, you'll be better at it if you get some education."

**EXERCISE 35-3**     **The colon**     To read about this topic, see section 35 in *Rules for Writers*, Sixth Edition.

In the following paragraphs, the italicized words indicate where two parts of a sentence come together. Decide whether the sentence needs a colon to join these parts. If so, insert it. If not, mark the spot "OK." The first spot has been done for you. Hint: You will need very few colons.

                                                  *OK*

Althea Gibson began playing *tennis when* she was a young teenager in the 1940s. In just over a decade, she *became one* of the world's greatest women tennis players.

The tennis world began to notice her after only a few years of amateur *play she* was winning women's singles meets one after the other. In 1950 and the years immediately *following, she* became more and more famous. By 1957, Althea Gibson, the rising young tennis star, was well known on both sides of the *Atlantic she* was the most respected woman player in Britain and America. In both countries, she won the national women's singles title two years in a row: 1957 and 1958. The British meet, which is *called Wimbledon,* is generally regarded *as the* unofficial world championship meet. Gibson also played on the US team at other major meets, *including the* Wightman Cup meet. That meet is a special British-American *meet that* pits US women against British women. When Althea Gibson was on the US team, the United States won.

Gibson's retirement from tennis in 1958 *was a* complete surprise to her fans. What reason did she give for her retirement? She had *decided to* become a professional golfer!

**EXERCISE 35-4**     **The colon: Guided review**

In the following paragraph, insert colons where they are needed and eliminate any improperly used colons. The numbers in the margins refer to appropriate rules in section 35 of *Rules for Writers*, Sixth Edition. The first revision has been done for you.

When the Eatons of North Carolina invited Althea Gibson to move into their home for the school year, she hesitated. Northerner Althea had one major fear/: white southerners. She decided to go in spite of her fears. At the Eatons' house, Althea had to get used to: wearing skirts, obeying rules, and getting along with people. She was expected to listen to adult conversations and join in with well-chosen comments. At the time, Althea considered these requirements to be serious disadvantages. However, there were also advantages to life with the Eatons, such as: regular meals, a room of her own, an allowance, and unlimited use of the doctor's private tennis court. School presented one overwhelming social problem Althea could not make friends with either boys or girls. The boys may have resented her athletic prowess and her self-confidence. The girls considered her a tomboy. Years later Althea still recalled their taunts "She's no lady" and "Look at her throwing that ball just like a man." Even the singing instructor added to her woes. When he placed her in the tenor section to make the chorus sound better, the other girls in the chorus could not control their giggles. Some people even made fun of her tennis, but her tenacity paid off. Before she had finished high school, Florida A & M University had offered her a scholarship. Althea had been right to expect problems if she lived in the South, but she had not anticipated what the problems would be. If she had put those high school years into a book, she could have titled it *The Unexpected, Problems Are Not Always What They Seem.*

*35a*

*35d*

*35d*

*35b*

*35a*

*35c*

## EXERCISE 36-1    The apostrophe: Guided practice

In the following paragraphs, add apostrophes where they are missing and delete or correct them where they have been misused. The numbers in the margin refer to appropriate rules in section 36 of *Rules for Writers*, Sixth Edition. The first revision has been done for you, and answers to this exercise appear in the back of the book.

During the 1990 troubles in Panama, American television and newspaper reporters had an exciting piece of news. They reported that for the first time American female soldiers had been engaged in actual combat. Acting as her ~~soldiers~~ *soldiers'* leader,    36a
Captain Linda Bray led her troops into combat. Names of two additional women who were involved in combat, Staff Sergeant April Hanley and PFC Christina Proctor, were reported in the newspapers. Their's were the only names reported, although    36e
other women also took part.

It wasn't the first time an American woman had fought in an American battle, but its not likely that many people are aware of that fact. The Civil War had its fe-    36c
male fighters too. Loreta Janeta Velazquez fought for the Confederates' in the Civil    36e
War after her husbands death. Like many other women whose husbands were killed    36a
in that war, she must have asked herself, "Whose going to take his place in battle?"    36c
The decision to fight was her's alone. Someone is sure to ask how that was possible,    36e
even in those days. Military identification was not very sophisticated in the 1860s.
Someones willingness to fight was that person's major qualification, and each fight-    36b
ing unit needed to replace it's losses as fast as possible. Velazquez simply disguised    36e
herself in mens clothing, found a troop needing replacements, and joined the fight.    36a
Loreta Janeta Velazquez was Linda Brays Civil War predecessor.    36a

**EXERCISE 36-2**    **The apostrophe**    To read about this topic, see section 36 in *Rules for Writers*, Sixth Edition.

A. Each of the following sentences has two words containing apostrophes. Only one of the apostrophes is used correctly in each sentence. Delete or move the other apostrophe. Example:

Further back in American history, one woman's soldiering had made her famous; no one has yet
had a story to match ~~her's.~~ *hers.*

1. Deborah Sampson never dreamed that she would someday fight in battles' for American independence, much less that the battles' outcomes might depend on her.

2. Because her parents' income was not enough to support their children, Deborah was sent to live with relatives of her parents' in another town.

3. Later she was sent to live in a foster family with ten sons'; the sons' acceptance of her was wholehearted, and one son became her fiancé when she grew up.

4. The Revolutionary War was'nt over when news of his death reached Deborah; she wasn't long in making a major decision.

5. Determined that his place should become her's, she enlisted under a man's name.

B. The following sentences contain no apostrophes. Add any that are needed. If a sentence is correct, mark it "OK." Example:

*Who's*      *who's*
~~Whose~~ to say ~~whos~~ right about Deborah Sampson's decision?

6. If men have the right to fight for their beliefs, should women have the right to fight for theirs?

7. Its clear that Deborah Sampson thought so; she enlisted twice to fight for hers.

8. On her first attempt, Sampson enlisted almost at the end of the day—and was discovered before its end arrived.

9. Though drinking was not a habit of hers, she spent her first evening as a soldier copying other new soldiers behavior.

10. Coming to the aid of this very noisy, very drunk, and very sick "buddy" of theirs, they soon were asking, "Whose this?"

**EXERCISE 36-3    The apostrophe    To read about this topic, see section 36 in *Rules for Writers*, Sixth Edition.**

Circle the correct form of the word in parentheses. The first one has been done for you.

Loreta Velazquez was not the only woman (who's / whose) help was used during the Civil War, nor was being a foot soldier the only way women served in that war.

She was not in combat, but Mary Walker, then in her (thirties / thirty's), served in the Union army. She served with such distinction that she became the first woman to receive the Medal of Honor, the (military's / militarys') highest-ranking medal. It is awarded only to members of the armed (forces / force's) and only for gallantry in action.

Mary (Walker's / Walkers) specialty was surgery. Just as shocking as her profession— the role of military surgeon was not (everyone's / everyones') idea of the proper role for a woman in the 1860s—were Dr. Walker's opinions on how women should dress. She said that women (shouldn't / should'nt) wear tight corsets because such corsets were injurious to (women's / womens') health. She even considered long skirts unhealthy. She felt so strongly on the subject of women's attire that she was determined to wear long pants. Army (regulations / regulations') did not permit such attire for a woman. (Who's / Whose) permission was required for her to do so? It required special permission from the US Congress, but Dr. Mary Walker finally won that battle of the Civil War.

She did not live to see the end of her final battle. After the war, she went back to her private practice of medicine and began fighting for a constitutional amendment to allow women to vote. Congress passed the Nineteenth Amendment in 1920. Unfortunately, Mary Walker died before (its / it's) adoption.

## EXERCISE 36-4    The apostrophe: Guided review

In the following paragraph, add apostrophes where they are missing and delete or correct them where they have been misused. The numbers in the margin refer to appropriate rules in section 36 of *Rules for Writers*, Sixth Edition. The first revision has been done for you.

Deborah Sampson, who fought in America's Revolution, fulfilled her light in-
fantryman duties pretending to be a private named Robert Shurtlieff. To ~~anyones~~ *anyone's*    36b
questions about where he was based, this private said, "West Point." Sampson's first
enlistment lasted less than a day, but her second enlistment was different. It lasted
until the wars end, and along with many others she was honorably discharged from    36a
the Continental army on October 23, 1783. Throughout her service, it was everyones opinion that she was an excellent soldier. Her officers reports on her were al-    36b, 36a
ways good. Wounded twice, she outwitted the doctors' and returned to her unit    36e
undetected; but when she came down with "the fevers," a doctor discovered the secret that until then had been her's alone. (Many of the distinctions among different    36e
illnesses that produce fevers—from typhoid to influenza—were not yet known; if pa-
tients had a high fever and it's accompanying discomforts for very long, they were    36e
diagnosed as having "the fevers.") Its no surprise that when her secret was finally    36c
told, her superior officers wouldnt believe it. Dressed in women's clothes, she was    36c
escorted to separate quarters not by the military police but by her superior officers.
Many years later, at Paul Reveres' suggestion, she donned the uniform again and    36a
went on speaking tours' to raise much-needed money for her family and to secure a    36e
monthly pension from the army she had once served.

## EXERCISE 37-1    Quotation marks: Guided practice

Edit the following sentences to correct the use of quotation marks and of punctuation with quotation marks. The numbers in the margin refer to appropriate rules in section 37 of *Rules for Writers*, Sixth Edition. Answers to this exercise appear in the back of the book. Example:

> **The parents watched as the doctor bandaged the boy's eyes. "For the love of God, what**
>
> **can we do ? " asked the father.**                                           37f

1.  The doctor answered "You can do nothing but pray."                         37f

2.  When the bandages were removed and the shades were opened to let in the
    bright sunlight, the doctor asked, "What do you see"?                        37f

3.  "Nothing," said the boy. I see nothing.                                      37a

4.  The village priest said "I have recently seen a remarkable school." He had just
    returned from a trip to Paris.                                              37f

5.  "In this school, he added blind students are taught to read."               37a

6.  "You didn't say "read," did you?" asked the boy's father.                   37c

7.  The boy responded to the priest's words as if they were a trick of some kind
    "Now you are joking with me. How can such a thing be possible?"             37f

8.  The boy, Louis, thought it would be "great fun" to visit that school someday. 37g

9.  His father promised "We will go soon, Louis."                              37f

10. And so it happened that ten-year-old Louis Braille entered the National
    Institute for Blind Youths and began the long effort to erase the fear people had
    of even the word blind.                                                    37e

**EXERCISE 37-2    Quotation marks**    To read about this topic, see section 37 in *Rules for Writers*, Sixth Edition.

Change each indirect quotation into a direct quotation, using correct punctuation and deleting or changing words as necessary. Example:

> **The doctor told them not to look for miracles.**
>
> *The doctor said, "Do not look for miracles."*

1.  The doctor added that in all probability their son would never see again.

2.  Mr. Braille exclaimed that he had seen blind students at the institute making their own clothes and shoes.

3.  The inventor of the military raised-dot system of writing told Louis to experiment all he wished but not to set his hopes too high.

4.  When his old friends in the village saw him with his stylus and paper, they asked him if he was still punching away at it.

5.  Louis asked the government official if he was blind and if he understood what it was like not to see.

**EXERCISE 37-3**     **Quotation marks**     To read about this topic, see section 37 in *Rules for Writers,* Sixth Edition.

---

In the following sentences, insert needed quotation marks and punctuation used with quotation marks. If a sentence is correct, mark it "OK." Example:

> One of Braille's students wrote, "Attending his classes was a pleasure to enjoy rather than a duty to fulfill."

1. Louis Braille asked the inventor of the military raised-dot system a serious question "Do you think it would be possible to change the symbols in some way, to reduce them in size?"

2. Barbier, the inventor of the system, replied "Of course. Anything is possible."

3. "I have hoped" said the founder of the institute "that this school would be a bright torch held aloft to bring light to the blind."

4. "I am going to instruct the teachers to begin using your system in the classroom," said the institute director. "You must understand, though, that your method has not yet been proved."

5. Louis Braille wanted a system so complete that people could read and write the words and music to a song like the Marseillaise, the French national anthem.

# EXERCISE 37-4    Quotation marks: Guided review

Edit the following paragraphs to correct the use of quotation marks and punctuation used with quotation marks. The numbers in the margin refer to appropriate rules in section 37 of *Rules for Writers*, Sixth Edition. The first revision has been done for you.

Louis Braille entered the National Institute for Blind Youths in Paris when he was ten. At twelve, he was already experimenting with a system of raised letters known as "night-~~writing~~," *writing,"* which was used by the military. Institute teachers decided    37f

that night-writing was impractical, but Louis became proficient at it. When Charles

Barbier, inventor of the system, visited the institute, Louis told him "Your symbols    37f

are too large and too complicated. Impressed, Barbier encouraged him and said that    37a

"since Louis was blind himself, he might discover the magic key that had eluded his    37g

teachers."

Louis Braille wanted a system that would work for everything from a textbook

on science to a poem like Heinrich Heine's Loreley. At fifteen, he had worked out his    37d

own system of six dots arranged in various patterns. "Read to me," he said to one of

his teachers, and I will take down your words." As the teacher read, Louis punched    37f

his paper and then read the passage back without error. The teacher exclaimed,

"Remarkable"! Government officials, not impressed enough to take any action, said    37f

simply that Braille should be encouraged. "You didn't say "encouraged," did you?"    37c

asked Braille. He wanted official acceptance, not simply encouragement. "The sys-

tem has proved itself," said Louis. We have been using it for five years now."    37f

For most people, the word Braille itself now means simply a system of reading    37e

and writing used by blind people; for blind people, it means freedom and independ-

ence. Braille himself died before his system was recognized beyond the institute. The

plaque on the house of his birth, however, records the world's recognition of his work

with these words: He opened the doors of knowledge to all those who cannot see.    37a

## EXERCISE 38-1    End punctuation: Guided practice

Supply end punctuation—period, quotation mark, or exclamation point—as needed in the following paragraphs. The numbers in the margin refer to appropriate rules in section 38 of *Rules for Writers*, Sixth Edition. The first and last revisions have been done for you, and answers to this exercise appear in the back of the book.

After Louis Braille invented his new system that would allow blind people to read and write, he tested it thoroughly. Students and faculty of the National       38a
Institute for Blind Youths were excited at how easily they could master it. They encouraged Louis to demonstrate the system to the French educational authorities, who made the rules for the institute Louis agreed to do so       38a, 38a

When Louis held the demonstration, all went well What excitement he and his       38a
friends felt But the authorities would not recommend that the institute adopt Louis's       38c
new system Why didn't the French authorities recognize the advantages of Braille's       38a
system Did they have a vested interest in the old system of teaching the blind Or a       38b, 38b
real doubt about the system Whatever their reasons, they delayed the pleasures of       38b
reading for thousands of people In addition, a new director, Dr. Pignier, even out-       38a
lawed the use of the system at the institute for four years       38a

Although unhappy and disheartened, Braille never gave up; he knew his system would enable the blind to read.       38a

**EXERCISE 38-2    End punctuation**    To read about this topic, see section 38 in
*Rules for Writers*, Sixth Edition.

Supply end punctuation—period, question mark, or exclamation point—for each of the following sentences. At least one sentence of each pair is a question. Example:

   a. Louis asked if he could demonstrate his technique at the institute.
                                                             *institute?"* ^
   b. Louis asked, "May I demonstrate my technique at the ~~institute"~~
                                                             ^

1a. What Louis had figured out was a new code

  b. What had Louis figured out

2a. What should I do about teaching it

  b. What to do about teaching it was the next decision to make

3a. Who could help him test the system was another question

  b. Who could help him test the system

4a. How extraordinary it was that a leatherworker's son should have such talent

  b. How was it that he had such extraordinary talent

5a. Why did he never give up, either as a child or as an adult

  b. Why he never gave up, either as a child or as an adult, puzzled many of his friends

## EXERCISE 38-3    End punctuation: Guided review

Supply appropriate end punctuation—period, question mark, or exclamation point—in the following paragraphs. The numbers in the margin refer to appropriate rules in section 38 of *Rules for Writers,* Sixth Edition. The first revision has been done for you.

Braille's system depended on a group of six dots. He called this group a "cell." He conceived of the cell as three rows with space for two dots on each row. But he did not have to put two dots on each row, and he did not have to use all three rows. Figuring it this way, Braille counted sixty-three possible arrangements for the    *38a*
dots. Using these possibilities, Braille worked out an alphabet. Then he added punctuation marks and numerals. But he still was not satisfied. There was something else that he wanted to do.

Braille knew very well that blindness does not keep someone from becoming proficient at a particular skill. Like many other blind people, Braille himself was an accomplished musician. As a young boy at the National Institute for Blind Youths, he had learned to play several instruments. But he could play only by ear Louis    *38a*
Braille wanted to be able to read music, play what he read, and then write music that other musicians could read and play.

When Braille was only fifteen, he devised a way to write music using his six-dot cell. As soon as he knew it was workable, he wanted a piano of his own to try it on. By saving his small salary, he was able to buy a piano. Next he wanted lessons Paris    *38a*
had many good music teachers. Braille took lessons from some of the best and then began to teach piano and violoncello at the institute. He also gave frequent piano recitals throughout Paris.

When he knew he was good on the piano, Braille said it was time to play something else "God's music," the church organ, was what he wanted to learn. With great    *38a*
effort he learned to manage the foot pedals, the double keyboard, and the rows of stops St. Nicholas-des-Champs Church hired him as organist. However, Braille    *38a*
found himself so busy thinking about stops and pedals that he couldn't keep up with the service at first. Did he resign Of course not Braille simply became so fa-    *38b, 38c*

miliar with the music that he did not have to think about it and could follow the church service as it went along Louis Braille may have been the first blind organist in Paris, but he was not the last. In Braille's lifetime, the institute's music director placed more than fifty blind organists in the city. 38a

Many people have wondered where Braille got the idea of adapting the Braille system to music. Did it come from one of his teachers Or one of his friends Or from his own mind? Whichever way it happened, the Braille system was adapted for music, and again Braille opened a new world to the blind. What an extraordinary gift this was Except for sight itself, could anyone have given blind musicians a greater gift 38b, 38b

38c

38b

*Note:* For all the exercises in section 39, you will need to refer to the following poem.

### The New Colossus

**by Emma Lazarus**

Not like the brazen giant of Greek fame,

With conquering limbs astride from land to land;

Here at our sea-washed, sunset gates shall stand

A mighty woman with a torch, whose flame

Is the imprisoned lightning, and her name

Mother of Exiles. From her beacon hand

Glows world-wide welcome; her mild eyes command

The air-bridged harbor that twin cities frame.

"Keep, ancient lands, your storied pomp!" cries she

With silent lips. "Give me your tired, your poor,

Your huddled masses yearning to breathe free,

The wretched refuse of your teeming shore,

Send these, the homeless, tempest-tost to me,

I lift my lamp beside the golden door."

## EXERCISE 39-1    Other punctuation marks: Guided practice

Edit the following paragraphs for correct use of the dash, parentheses, brackets, ellipsis mark, and slash. Refer to the poem "The New Colossus" (p. 143) as necessary. The numbers in the margin refer to appropriate rules in section 39 of *Rules for Writers*, Sixth Edition. The first revision has been done for you, and answers to this exercise appear in the back of the book.

The most famous woman in America is Miss Liberty a 450,000-pound, 154-foot    *39a*
resident of New York City. For people all over the world, the Statue of Liberty symbolizes America. Yet the idea for the statue came not from America, England, or even
New York itself, but from France. Three men can claim the credit for construction of    *39a*
Miss Liberty: 1. Frédéric-Auguste Bartholdi, sculptor; 2. Alexandre-Gustave Eiffel,    *39b*
structural engineer; and 3. Richard Morris Hunt, architect. France gave the statue
to the United States, and the United States provided the pedestal—on which it    *39a*
stands.

Two Americans contributed significantly to the statue. The first was Joseph
Pulitzer, then owner and publisher of the *New York World* (and a Russian immi-    *39b*
grant). He led several fundraising efforts and urged every American to give what
he/she could to help build the pedestal. The second American who contributed sig-    *39e*
nificantly was Emma Lazarus. She wrote the famous lines on the bronze plaque inside the statue. Her three-word title "The New Colossus" (which means "huge
statue") alludes to a statue built in the harbor of Rhodes in ancient Greece. The most
quoted lines from "The New Colossus" are probably these: "Give me your tired, your
poor, / Your huddled masses yearning to breathe free."

**EXERCISE 39-2**    **Other punctuation marks**    To read about this topic, see section 39 in *Rules for Writers*, Sixth Edition.

Edit the following sentences by using the punctuation indicated in brackets. Refer to the poem "The New Colossus" (p. 143) as necessary. Example:

Bartholdi's Statue of Liberty ‸better known in France as Liberty Enlightening the World ‸celebrated ideals that France and America shared. [Dashes]

1.  America's Revolution celebrated liberty. The French added two more words to form the battle cry of the French Revolution, "Liberty, Equality, and Fraternity." [Dash]

2.  Emma Lazarus understood Bartholdi's desire to demonstrate this common interest. In her opening line, "Not like the brazen giant of Greek fame" (the Colossus of Rhodes), she alludes to an ancient statue one hundred feet high. [Brackets]

3.  Bartholdi was determined to build "A mighty woman—Mother of Exiles" and place her in New York Harbor. [Ellipsis mark]

4.  He traveled all over America, to Boston, Chicago, Denver, Salt Lake City, and many other places, to promote his idea. [Dashes]

5.  He was amazed at the country's size, industry, and enthusiasm for creating things, buildings, that is, not art. [Parentheses]

6.  Bartholdi discovered that money, the enthusiasm of US citizens, and political support, all necessary for his project, were hard to get. [Parentheses]

7.  He decided on a novel, hands-on approach, allowing people to climb into completed parts of the statue. [Dash]

8.  Three cities were chosen: [1] In Philadelphia, the hand and torch attracted Centennial Exhibition visitors; [2] in New York, the same exhibit drew people downtown; and [3] in Paris, visitors explored the head and shoulders. [Parentheses]

9.  When more money was needed, wealthy newspaper publisher Joseph Pulitzer, an immigrant himself, turned to nonwealthy Americans, working-class men, women, and children, and it was their small gifts that paid for the statue's pedestal. [Dashes]

10. Their gifts allowed Miss Liberty's torch to shine out over the water to say, "Send these, the homeless, tempest-tost to me, I lift my lamp beside the golden door." [Slash]

## EXERCISE 39-3    Other punctuation marks    To read about this topic, see section
39 in *Rules for Writers*, Sixth Edition.

The dashes, parentheses, brackets, ellipsis marks, and slashes in the following sentences are not well used. Edit the sentences to be more effective by deleting punctuation marks, replacing them with other marks, or restructuring the sentences. Refer to "The New Colossus" (p. 143) as necessary. Example:

> On October 29, 1886, one hundred and ten years after the Declaration of Independence, Miss Liberty was formally dedicated.

1. Miss Liberty was the only woman at her dedication (except for two Frenchwomen who came with the sculptor).

2. On that day, the Lady whose "beacon hand/Glow(ed) world-wide welcome" was almost obscured from view by rain and wind.

3. Also, the crowds of people pushing and shoving resembled the ". . . huddled masses" Emma Lazarus wrote about.

4. The crowd—crushed together—trying to listen to the main speaker—he was William M. Evarts—could hear other voices too.

5. Women who were angry about being excluded from the ceremony had sailed in close to the island (they had chartered a boat) and were yelling their protests.

6. With all of the noise from the crowd and/or the women, the speaker paused.

7. He paused so long that an aide thought the speech was over. The aide signaled Bartholdi (who had been waiting inside the statue).

8. Bartholdi saw the signal and unveiled the statue . . . an hour early.

9. The plaque with Emma Lazarus's poem on it was not on the statue at this time; it was added later—in 1903—without any special attention.

10. It is still there today for all visitors to read/ponder as they meet America's most beloved lady.

## EXERCISE 39-4    Other punctuation marks: Guided review

Edit the following paragraphs for the most effective use of the dash, parentheses, brackets, ellipsis mark, and slash. Refer to "The New Colossus" (p. 143) as necessary. The numbers in the margin refer to appropriate rules in section 39 of *Rules for Writers,* Sixth Edition. The first revision has been done for you.

*fourteen-line*

The sonnet is a poem ~~/ of fourteen lines /~~ with a particular pattern to its                    *39a*

rhymes; it is often used to compare or contrast two items. Emma Lazarus's poem

"The New Colossus" is a sonnet. Lazarus uses its fourteen lines to contrast two stat-

ues. The ancient Colossus of Rhodes (which was male) represented the sun god; the          *39b*

new Colossus was female and represented Liberty. The Rhodes Colossus symbolized

what Lazarus calls "storied pomp." The French-made American one stood for free-

dom and opportunity.

In her first line, "Not like the brazen (bronze) giant of Greek fame," Lazarus          *39c*

refers to the material of which the old Colossus was made. Bronze, a valuable metal

when the Colossus of Rhodes was erected in 280 BC, was available only to the

wealthy. Miss Liberty was made of copper, a material available to all classes of

people. When Miss Liberty was erected in 1898, America's least valuable coin—the       *39a*

one-cent piece, was made from copper. Miss Liberty was for everyone, not just the

wealthy.

The major contrast Lazarus sets up is in the attitudes of the two statues. The

old Colossus is powerful, not caring about the ". . . wretched refuse" of its "teeming      *39d*

shore." The new one welcomes all: "Send these, the homeless, tempest-tost to me, I      *39e*

lift my lamp beside the golden door."

## REVIEW OF 32–39: Punctuation

Edit the following paragraphs to correct errors in punctuation or to use more effective punctuation. Refer to the poem "The New Colossus" (p. 143) as necessary. The numbers in the margin refer to appropriate rules in sections 32–39 of *Rules for Writers*, Sixth Edition. The first revision has been done for you.

The outside of the Statue of Liberty is made of copper, but what is inside the | 32a

statue. Inside the statue are: iron braces and staircases. The thin copper plates that | 38d, 35d

form the outside of the statue are bolted to a network of iron braces. There are sev-

eral staircases allowing workers and tourists to climb all the way into the head and

the torch. (This intricate network of braces and stairways was designed by

Alexandre-Gustave Eiffel; the same man who designed the famous Eiffel Tower in | 34d

Paris.)

For some years, the lighting equipment for Miss Libertys torch was also inside. | 36a

Soon after the statue was set up for example engineers tried Edison's new invention, | 32f

the electric lightbulb. They cut holes in the torch's copper sheets and hung light-

bulbs inside. Later, the copper sheets came down and glass windows went up.

Giving Miss Liberty a light that everyone would recognize as hers, challenged engi- | 33g

neers and designers for sixty more years. When the statue was restored in the 1980s | 32b

part of the lighting equipment went outside. Floodlights were installed on the torch's

balcony, and focused on thin gold sheets that form the torch ". . . whose flame / Is | 33a, 39d

the imprisoned lightning. Miss Liberty will be able to welcome newcomers for many | 37a

years.

## EXERCISE 40/41/42-1    Abbreviations, numbers, and italics: Guided practice

Correct any errors in abbreviations, numbers, and italics in the following paragraphs. The numbers in the margin refer to appropriate rules in sections 40–42 of *Rules for Writers*, Sixth Edition. The first revision has been done for you, and a suggested revision of these paragraphs appears in the back of the book.

Everyone has heard of Christopher Columbus, but not many people know
much about him. Most people learn that he discovered America in ~~1492 AD.~~ Some
AD 1492.
^ 40c
people know that he had three ships, and they might be able to name them. (The
ships were the "Niña," the "Pinta," and the "Santa María.") A few people might even    42b
remember that Columbus thought he had found the Indies. And those with great
self-confidence might be willing to guess at the number of trips he made to his India.
(It was 4.) Probably no one could tell you his favorite word, adelante.    41a, 42d

If they were asked what Columbus was trying to prove with his expensive journey, most people would reply that he was trying to prove the world is round. They would be wrong. If they were asked what Columbus meant by "the Indies," they would probably say "India." They would be wrong again. If they were asked what Columbus's rank was, they would most likely say "captain." They would be wrong again. If they were asked what his sailors feared most, a no. of them would reply,    40e
"They feared that the boats would fall off the edge of the earth." And they would be
wrong *again.*    42e

Isn't it strange that people can be so ignorant about a well-known man like Columbus?

## EXERCISE 40/41/42-2  Abbreviations and numbers   To read about this topic, see sections 40 and 41 in *Rules for Writers*, Sixth Edition.

A.  Edit the following sentences to correct errors in the use of abbreviations. Mark the one correct sentence "OK." Example:

The sailors who went with Columbus had the same four directions sailors still use: *north, south, east, and west.*
~~N, S, E, and W.~~
  ^

1.  Sailors in AD 1492 knew the world was round; they were not afraid of sailing off the edge of the world.

2.  They worried about more serious things—e.g., whether the wind would blow both ways so they could get back home to Spain.

3.  They also weren't sure about distances; however, one famous Italian prof., Dr. Toscanelli, thought he knew.

4.  He was willing to estimate the distance from Lisbon, Port., to Japan.

5.  He said that the exact no. of miles between the two places was three thousand nautical miles.

B.  Edit the following sentences to correct errors in the use of numbers. Mark the one correct sentence "OK." Example:

                    *three*
Dr. Toscanelli set the distance at ~~3~~ thousand nautical miles.
                      ^

6.  In twelve ninety-eight, Marco Polo had written a book about his travels to the Indies.

7.  7,448 islands were in the Indies, according to Marco Polo's book.

8.  Columbus was 41 when he convinced Queen Isabella to send him to find those islands.

9.  As part of the contract, Columbus demanded ten % of the treasure he brought back to Spain.

10. At 8:00 a.m. on August 3, 1492, Columbus set out from Spain for the Indies.

**EXERCISE 40/41/42-3    Italics (underlining)**    To read about this topic, see section 42 in *Rules for Writers*, Sixth Edition.

Edit the following sentences to correct the use of italics (underlining). Example:

**Marco Polo's book was named <u>Description of the World</u>.**

1. On the "Niña," the "Pinta," and the "Santa María," Columbus had one hundred men, all kinds of supplies, and enough cats to control the rat population.

2. Columbus always spoke the same word to his men—Adelante! (That means "Forward!" or "Sail on!")

3. Marco Polo's book had not prepared the men for seeing the same horizon week after week, seemingly ad infinitum.

4. To every fear or complaint, Columbus simply replied "Forward!" and that word forward began to get on the sailors' nerves.

5. Columbus offered a special reward—a silk jacket—to the first man who spotted *land.*

# EXERCISE 40/41/42-4    Abbreviations, numbers, and italics: Guided review

Correct any errors in the use of abbreviations, numbers, and italics in the following paragraphs. The numbers in the margin refer to appropriate rules in sections 40–42 of *Rules for Writers,* Sixth Edition. The first revision has been done for you.

Columbus's first voyage, in 1492 ~~AD~~ **AD**, was successful. Pleased with the gifts he had brought and impressed by his reports, King Ferdinand and Queen Isabella quickly ordered him to organize another voyage. Columbus was delighted to do so. At first his luck held. Led by the flagship Maríagalante, a fleet of 17 ships and a thousand men who wanted to colonize the new land made the second trip in twenty-one days. Columbus's good fortune, however, did not last. Life went downhill for the Italian sailor from that time on.

*40c*

*42b, 41a*

The so-called Admiral of the Ocean Sea (a title Columbus had given himself) had one disastrous experience after another. When he got back to the recently settled new town he had left, the whole settlement had been destroyed, and the 39 men he had left there were all dead. Columbus quickly found a new spot for his new colony, the first European colony in America. The new site had serious drawbacks; e.g., bad water and many mosquitoes. Embarrassed, Columbus had to send Queen Isabella's ships back for help; he loaded them not with gold but with pepper, sandalwood, and a no. of exotic birds.

*41a*

*40d*

*40e*

Other voyages followed, but each turned out worse than the one before it. Not even his favorite word, *adelante,* seemed to work for Columbus anymore. His first voyage had definitely been the most successful.

## EXERCISE 43/44/45-1 Spelling, the hyphen, and capital letters: Guided practice

Edit the following paragraphs to correct misspellings and errors in the use of the hyphen and capital letters. The numbers in the margin refer to appropriate rules in sections 43–45 of *Rules for Writers*, Sixth Edition. The first revision has been done for you, and a revision of these paragraphs appears in the back of the book.

Columbus's return to Spain from his first exploration was difficult. The *Niña*

*separated,*

and the *Pinta* were ~~seperated,~~ the *Niña* almost sank, and the governor on the island        43d

                        ^

of Santa María put Columbus's whole crew in jail. It seemed a miracle that both

boats arrived in the harbor at Palos on the same day.

As difficult as that return was, the reception at court quite made up for it.

Columbus certainly made an all out effort to impress the court, the city, and the en-       44d

tire country. Lavishly attired, he recieved a grand welcome as he led his entourage       43c

into Barcelona, the spanish capital. It must have been a sight to behold: A proces-       45a, 45f

sion like none Barcelona had ever seen before. Leading the parade was a gaudily be-

decked horse carrying Columbus, followed by six captive "indians" and all the crew.       45a

Everyone but Columbus was carrying boxes, baskets, and cages full of interesting

and exotic items.

When the group reached the throne room, King Ferdinand and Queen Isabella

stood up to greet Columbus formally and to admire his apron covered captives.       44b

Columbus asked the royal couple to except gifts of plants, shells, darts, thread, and       43b

gold. As intrigued as they were with the other gifts, King Ferdinand and Queen

Isabella basicly wanted gold. Luckily, Columbus had collected enough samples of it       43d

to satisfy them.

By the end of the first week home, Columbus had such prestige that everyone

wanted to accomodate the wishes of the Italian sailor at the court of Spain. Columbus       43d

had no doubt that he would receive a Commission for a second voyage of exploration       45a

or even colonization.

## EXERCISE 43/44/45-2     Spelling     To read about this topic, see section 43 in
*Rules for Writers,* Sixth Edition.

Edit the following sentences to correct spelling errors. (Hint: There are ten errors.) Example:

Others may have considered him ~~incredibally~~ *incredibly* lucky, but Columbus ~~beleived~~ *believed* he had been called by God to be the one to find a new way to the Indies.

1. To begin with, he was born in Genoa, Italy, the best place concievable for someone who wanted to be in the sailing busness, since Genoa was a major seaport.

2. Other people said his being born there was all "just chance"; Columbus prefered to think that it was part of God's arrangment for him.

3. He was not suprised to be the sole survivor of a shipwreck that occured when he was twenty-five.

4. Weather others excepted the idea or not, Columbus knew he survived such a disasterous event because God had plans for him.

5. He thought that even his name emphasized his calling: *Christopher* means "Christ-bearing," and he would take Christ's name to the "heatherns" in India.

**EXERCISE 43/44/45-3**   **The hyphen**   To read about this topic, see section 44 in *Rules for Writers,* Sixth Edition.

The writer of the following sentences got hyphen-happy. Remove six of the eleven hyphens. If a sentence needs no hyphens removed, mark it "OK." Example:

> Columbus's all-consuming goal made him think that God͜himself had worked͜out the fortuitous marriage Columbus made in 1478.

1. Marrying into a noble-family when he was thirty-three gave Columbus direct-access to the king of Portugal.

2. When the king firmly-declined Columbus's request to finance an exploratory-voyage, this well-known sailor decided he was supposed to go to Spain.

3. Queen Isabella was anxious to make everyone into a practicing-Christian; because Columbus was religious, she did not consider the voyage a half-witted proposal.

4. After his discovery of "India," Columbus received confirmation of his self-given title, Admiral of the Ocean Seas and Viceroy of the Indies.

5. When the *Santa María* was wrecked, Columbus saw the incident as his God-given opportunity to go back posthaste to Spain, get more men, and return to this newly-found land.

**EXERCISE 43/44/45-4**     **Capital letters**     To read about this topic, see section 45 in *Rules for Writers*, Sixth Edition.

---

Edit the following paragraphs to correct errors in capitalization. The first sentence has been edited for you. You should find ten more errors.

If Columbus had made his return trip first, he might not have been so eager to set out
for the ~~indies~~. The voyage turned out all right, but it had its bad times.
    *Indies.*

To begin with, the *Niña* and the *Pinta* were separated on the way back to Spain. The weather was very bad, especially when the two ships ran into a storm west of the Azores. The *Niña* almost sank. Columbus was so sure it was going down that he put a record of his Discoveries in a small barrel, sealed it completely, and threw it overboard. That way, if the ship went down, there was still a chance that someone would learn of his discoveries. Actually, the ship made it to Santa María, a portuguese island. The governor there thought Columbus was lying about his adventures and arrested the crew. The crew was released only because Columbus threatened to shoot up the town.

The *Niña* was thrown off course again, but then Columbus's luck turned. The boat came into Lisbon, and Columbus was a guest of king John II for a brief time before he took off for Spain again. finally, the *Niña* made it home. On March 15, 1493, it sailed into the Harbor at Palos. The *Pinta* arrived shortly afterward on the same day. Such a coincidence certainly seemed to be a sign of divine approval and delighted Columbus. When queen Isabella saw what Columbus had brought back, she was impressed. She thought that god had surely had a hand in the matter. Certainly many influences had played a part in his success that Spring. Even Marco Polo's book *Description of the world* had played a role: Getting Columbus started on the journey. Columbus was convinced that his life was just one miracle after another. "i've been chosen," he might have said. "God has chosen me."

## EXERCISE 43/44/45-5    Spelling, the hyphen, and capital letters: Guided review

Correct any errors in spelling or in use of the hyphen or capital letters in the following paragraphs. The numbers in the margin refer to appropriate rules in sections 43–45 of *Rules for Writers*, Sixth Edition. The first revision has been done for you.

After being feted, feasted, and honored on his return from his first voyage
across the ocean, Columbus must have told and ~~re-told~~ *retold* the story of his trip. He                  44a
would have told listeners how, after the ships had sailed for twenty one days, his                  44c
men threatened to turn back because they had never sailed so far west before.
Columbus, sure of his special calling as an explorer, promised them that they would
sight land within three days. On the evening of the third day, at ten o'clock, he
thought he saw a light and alerted a nearby servant. Both of them lost sight of it almost at once. But at two o'clock the next morning, a cannon shot sounded from the
*Pinta.* "Land! Land!" cried the sailors. Columbus had kept his promise. No wonder
he began to sign his name with a secret code to show that he was more special then                  43b
other people.

Retelling the story of his voyage, Columbus would have described the beautiful
Island that the ships first landed on. He named it San Salvador. He would have told                  45a
how, at every island he and his men visited, natives had flocked to the boats to see
the strangers. One day, more than a thousand people had come in just one hour.
Columbus had spent three months exploring and setting up a fort before leaving for
the return trip to Spain. And on their return, eight months later, he and his crew
had recieved a royal welcome.                  43c

Yes, he had had a few problems on the trip out, and the return trip had been
very hard, but one set of memories was indelibly imprinted on Columbus's brain:
The memories of that remarkably successful first voyage.                  45f

## REVIEW OF 40–45: Mechanics

This essay has eleven errors in spelling and mechanics. The numbers in the margin refer to appropriate rules in sections 40–45 of *Rules for Writers,* Sixth Edition. The first revision has been done for you. Find and correct ten more errors.

Columbus made an all‿out effort to find the Indies—India, China, the East     *44d*

Indies, and Japan. Instead, he found Cuba, Venezuela, the Bahamas, and the coasts

of South and Central America. Unable to find gold, he captured 5 hundred natives     *41a*

and had them shipped back to Spain to be sold as slaves. He punished the natives

so severely when they did not bring him gold that in two years one third of them ran     *44c*

away or were killed or sold. Things went from bad to worse; e.g., many settlers died     *40d*

of illness, and some went back to Spain with bad reports of his governance.

Convinced that God was unhappy with him for some transgression, Columbus re-

turned to Spain wearing a monk's course garb and walking humbly. People gave him     *43b*

a new title, Columbus, admiral of the Mosquitoes.     *45b*

Ferdinand and Isabella gave him another opportunity, though, and on May

thirtieth, 1498, Columbus set out again. The voyage was a disaster, with Columbus     *41b*

ending up back in Spain, this time in chains. Columbus got one more chance, but

hurricanes and storms plagued him. He wrote, "other tempests have I seen, but     *45e*

none so long or so grim as this." He must by now have realized that Dr. Toscanelli

did not no his geography very well. Yet "Sail on!" was still his answer to *every* set-     *43b, 42e*

back.

When Columbus got back to Spain, sick and exhausted, queen Isabella died be-     *45b*

fore he could see her. Columbus died still insisting he had found the Indies. He had

not, of course. He had done far more: He had discovered a new world.

**EXERCISE 62-1**     **Parts of speech: Preview**     To read about this topic, see section 62 in *Rules for Writers*, Sixth Edition.

---

In the following paragraphs, label the part of speech of each italicized word. Use these codes: noun (N), pronoun (PN), helping verb (HV), main verb (MV), adjective (ADJ), adverb (ADV), preposition (P), conjunction (C). The first word has been marked for you, and answers to this exercise appear in the back of the book.

     America's Declaration of Independence *seems* [MV] very formal to today's *readers*. Many of its sentences *are* long and involved, and some *of* its words seem old fashioned. But *its* central message is loud *and* clear to all those who take the time to read and understand it, whether they are schoolchildren *or* adult immigrants.

     Those somewhat *formal* words contain both a declaration and a promise. The Declaration *starts* with a seventy-one word statement called the "Preamble." It *simply* says that when one group of people break their ties *with* another, those people *should* tell *everyone* their reasons for breaking up.

     In the next part, called the "Declaration of Rights," the colonists list their basic assumptions *about* life—that everyone is born with *certain* rights ("life, liberty, and the pursuit of happiness"), that governments have power only *when* people give it to *them*, and that when a government repeatedly *acts* in ways that deny people's rights, people have a right and a duty to overthrow that *government* and build another one.

     It was a *bold* beginning for a bold document—a declaration promising freedom that has *been* celebrated by Americans for more than two hundred years.

**EXERCISE 62-2**    **Nouns and noun/adjectives**    To read about this topic, see section 62a in *Rules for Writers,* Sixth Edition.

A.  Each of the following word groups contains only one noun. Circle the noun. Example:

| national | nationwide | (nation) |

1. defendable    defend    defenses

2. speaking    speaker    speak

3. just    justice    justly

4. normal    normally    normality

5. repetition    repeating    repeated

B.  Underline each noun (including noun/adjectives) in the following sentences. Example:

**When they apply for American <u>citizenship</u>, <u>refugee</u> <u>immigrants</u> must study some famous American <u>documents</u>.**

6.  Schoolchildren and new citizens have similar homework assignments.

7.  They both must learn the pledge of allegiance to the country's flag.

8.  Many of these people also memorize the opening words of the Declaration of Independence.

9.  The Preamble to the Constitution is often assigned, as well as some famous speeches and the national anthem.

10. If students pass their tests on all of this, they are promoted; if immigrants pass theirs, they are welcomed into American citizenship.

## EXERCISE 62-3    Nouns and noun/adjectives    To read about this topic, see section 62a in *Rules for Writers*, Sixth Edition.

All of the following paired sentences contain some form of the word *exhibit.* In each pair, circle the letter of the sentence that uses the word *exhibit* as a noun or noun/adjective, and be prepared to explain how you know it is a noun. (Hint: There is only one noun/adjective.) Example:

(a.) The Declaration of Independence is on exhibit at the National Archives in Washington, DC.

 b. The Archives exhibit the Declaration of Independence for many tourist groups.

1a. Many people do not realize that the exhibits in the national museums change frequently.

 b. Each museum exhibits a wide variety of materials.

2a. Museums can exhibit something of interest to almost any visitor.

 b. It is impossible to predict which exhibit any one visitor will enjoy.

3a. Most children prefer an interactive exhibit over any other kind.

 b. The children can exhibit their own skill in operating the interactive devices.

4a. Most of the exhibit halls have excellent signs and explanations about what the visitor can see.

 b. Curators can exhibit rare items safely in specially constructed cases.

5a. When the museums are exhibiting items borrowed from another place, visitors have a limited time to visit the displays.

 b. When exhibits contain items from other collections, however, many more people can see and enjoy those items.

**EXERCISE 62-4** **Pronouns and pronoun/adjectives** To read about this topic, see section 62b in *Rules for Writers*, Sixth Edition.

A. Circle the five pronouns in each group of words. Example:

(his) (they) under (whoever) (no one) (themselves)

| | | | | | |
|---|---|---|---|---|---|
| 1. I | she | of | he | ours | everyone |
| 2. her | me | it | to | whose | many |
| 3. for | him | you | us | this | someone |
| 4. they | my | that | we | from | some |
| 5. in | them | mine | your | these | nothing |
| 6. at | yours | her | his | all | none |
| 7. hers | our | its | nobody | another | over |
| 8. under | myself | their | yours | each | several |
| 9. from | theirs | who | which | either | something |
| 10. whom | those | any | both | few | through |

B. Underline the pronouns (including pronoun/adjectives) in the following sentences. Except in the example, there are two in each sentence. Example:

<u>Our</u> Declaration of Independence includes <u>these</u> famous words: "<u>We</u> hold <u>these</u> truths to be self-evident."

11. Whoever reads the Declaration of Independence finds a message for everyone.

12. One of its basic premises is the equality of people.

13. Furthermore, the Declaration declares, "They are endowed by their Creator with certain un-alienable rights."

14. "Among these are life, liberty, and the pursuit of happiness" may be its most famous line.

15. Refugees who apply for citizenship are claiming those rights.

## EXERCISE 62-5    Verbs    To read about this topic, see section 62c in *Rules for Writers*, Sixth Edition.

A.  All of the following paired sentences contain some form of the word *promise*. In each pair, circle the letter of the sentence that uses a form of the word *promise* as a verb. (Hint: The words *promised* and *promising* can sometimes function as adjectives.) Example:

> a. The founders of this country made certain promises to each other.
>
> (b.) Each document of this country promises special things to the people who live here.

1a.  In a way, the Constitution is a set of promises.

 b.  The government promises to do certain things for citizens.

2a.  In turn, the citizens must promise to obey certain laws.

 b.  The citizens' promise is just as important as the government's.

3a.  Some early citizens thought the Constitution had not promised them enough rights.

 b.  They thought that the promised rights were not specific enough.

4a.  By adding a Bill of Rights to the Constitution, citizens demanded a promise about freedom of religion.

 b.  The Bill of Rights does indeed promise freedom of religion.

5a.  One of the most promising signs of political health in the colonies was their insistence on gaining certain rights.

 b.  Whenever citizens repeat their oath of allegiance, they are promising anew to honor the Constitution.

B.  Underline all verbs in the paragraph below and label them MV (main verb) or HV (helping verb) above the line. The first sentence has been done for you.

       *HV    MV*

Who <u>should</u> <u>vote</u>? All citizens should go to the polls and vote. When citizens do this, they are making important choices that can affect their lives and the lives of others. In addition, citizens must tell their elected representatives how they feel about certain issues. If the representatives ignore these messages, they may lose their jobs. It is important that these representatives stay in touch with the voters, but it is just as important that the voters send messages. Without this kind of communication, America's great democratic experiment will fail.

**EXERCISE 62-6     Adjectives and adverbs**     To read about this topic, see sections
62d and 62e in *Rules for Writers*, Sixth Edition.

---

A.  Label each of the following words as an adjective (ADJ) or an adverb (ADV). You should find
    twelve adjectives and eight adverbs. Example:

    clean ___ADJ___

1.  inexpensive _____        8.  beautiful _____        15.  rich _____

2.  very _____              9.  sometimes _____        16.  lonely _____

3.  rude _____             10.  political _____        17.  oily _____

4.  not _____              11.  ten _____              18.  slowly _____

5.  crazy _____            12.  never _____            19.  always _____

6.  lovely _____           13.  tired _____            20.  common _____

7.  extremely _____        14.  aloud _____

B.  Label the adjectives (ADJ) and adverbs (ADV) in the following sentences. Ignore the articles
    *a, an,* and *the.* You should find ten adjectives and five adverbs. Example:

                                        ADJ              ADV      ADJ
    **The Constitution and the Bill of Rights are separate, but they go together as a single document.**

21.  The Bill of Rights is the ten amendments that immediately follow the Constitution.

22.  The First Amendment is the most familiar of the famous rights.

23.  It guarantees religious freedom and freedom of speech for American citizens.

24.  It also guarantees freedom of the press, an extremely important freedom in a democratic
     country.

25.  Because representatives to the original Congress valued the right to discuss legislation pub-
     licly, the Bill of Rights assures citizens of the right to hold meetings and to petition the fed-
     eral government.

**EXERCISE 62-7**    **Prepositions**    To read about this topic, see section 62f in *Rules for Writers,* Sixth Edition.

A.  Many prepositions express opposite ideas. Fill in the blanks below with prepositions that express the opposite idea to the one listed. Examples:

like *unlike*_____          into *out of*_____

1.  above _____          6.  after _____

2.  against _____          7.  down _____

3.  in _____          8.  inside _____

4.  on _____          9.  over _____

5.  to _____          10.  with _____

B.  Circle all twenty prepositions in the following paragraph.

The men who wrote the Declaration of Independence dealt with many political controversies. In addition, they disagreed about many ideas. During their discussions, some still felt they should come to terms with England, some insisted on giving all of the reasons for their break with England, and some were against war under the existing circumstances. They argued over these issues frequently, making agreement seem impossible at first. They stuck to their task despite many disagreements between individuals, and in the end they put their feelings into words that remain famous today.

## EXERCISE 62-8    Prepositions and conjunctions    To read about this topic, see
sections 62f and 62g in *Rules for Writers*, Sixth Edition.

---

In the following sentences, label all prepositions (P), coordinating conjunctions (CC), and subordinating conjunctions (SUB). The numbers in the brackets after each sentence indicate how many of each you should find. Example:

SUB     P                 P            CC       P
When the Bill of Rights was adopted, it gave to American citizens rights and guarantees none of the
         CC
colonists or their predecessors had enjoyed. [3P, 2CC, 1SUB]

1. When the founders of the United States wrote the Bill of Rights, they were recalling their past troubles with England. [3P, 1SUB]

2. They were also hoping that this new country and its laws would be different. [1CC, 1SUB]

3. Before the American Revolution, English officers and their men had been quartered in colonists' homes. [2P, 1CC]

4. The colonists often objected, but they could do nothing about the situation. [1P, 1CC]

5. Although they petitioned and appealed, nothing changed. [1CC, 1SUB]

6. Because the colonists objected to this practice, they put a special amendment about it in the Bill of Rights. [4P, 1SUB]

7. That amendment says that the government cannot make people give free room and board to soldiers unless the country is at war. [2P, 1CC, 2SUB]

8. Another problem was that, although the colonists objected, under English rule they and their homes could be searched by any magistrate or his appointees. [2P, 2CC, 2SUB]

9. Another amendment to the Bill of Rights would protect citizens from unreasonable searches; searching a citizen's home would require a warrant. [3P]

10. Because the Bill of Rights was added to the Constitution, Americans are still protected from these and several other intrusions by the government. [4P, 1CC, 1SUB]

**EXERCISE 62-9**     **Parts of speech: Review**     To read about this topic, see section 62 of *Rules for Writers,* Sixth Edition.

---

In the following paragraph, label the parts of speech of the italicized words. Use these codes: noun (N), pronoun (PN), helping verb (HV), main verb (MV), adjective (ADJ), adverb (ADV), preposition (P), conjunction (C). The first word has been marked for you.

Americans fought a long *hard* war to secure the freedoms and rights that *their* Declaration had proclaimed. Even *while* the war was going on, France (America's ally) *was* trying to get America to agree *to* a truce. France proposed a treaty that *would* give America its independence *without* any questions. But under the French *proposal,* the boundaries of America would be established *by* which country's army was *currently* in control of the land. That would give Spain *and* France control of major portions *of* the land Americans claimed. John Adams, America's *negotiator,* refused to discuss such a plan.

Adams was simply carrying out the spirit of the Declaration that had started the war. In the final *section* of their Declaration of Independence, the Americans had *used* another impossibly long sentence—more than one hundred words—to declare their separation from Great Britain and their determination to make their own decisions. They could *not* then have known how *costly* defending that Declaration would be. *But* when the war was over, the colonists had won the rights for which *they* had pledged to each other their lives, their fortunes, and their *sacred* honor.

**EXERCISE 63-1**     **Sentence patterns: Preview**     To read about this topic, see section 63 in *Rules for Writers*, Sixth Edition.

Label the function of each italicized word or word group in the following paragraphs. Use these codes: subject (S), verb (V), subject complement (SC), direct object (DO), indirect object (IO), and object complement (OC). The first sentence has been done for you, and answers to this exercise appear in the back of the book.

               *S*           *V*       *DO*

New art *forms* often *lead* the *public* to a new way of looking at things. Frequently, however, viewers are not yet ready to understand the new forms.

A *group* of French artists *had* this *problem* in the 1800s. These artists completely changed their way of painting. Instead of painting in the subdued, dark tones of a formal studio, *they* often *went* outdoors. One of their new techniques was the use of color. *They* nearly always *gave* their *paintings* great *bursts* of color like sunlight on a field. Art *lovers* in France *were surprised* by such bright colors on the artists' canvases. People often called such paintings "open-air paintings." These *artists* usually *made* even their indoor *scenes* very *bright* with light and colors. Through an open window onto a bouquet of flowers or a bright-haired child *would pour* bright *sunshine*. *Were* Pierre-Auguste Renoir's *paintings* always *bright* and *cheerful?* Yes, and those of Claude Monet, Camille Pissarro, and Paul Cézanne were equally pleasant. These *painters*, now called "impressionists," *are admired* all over the world today, but in their own time the artists had to educate their viewers.

Twentieth-century artists had the same problem. Two new art *forms* from that period *are* good *examples*, "op art" and "pop art." *Both* of these *showed* their *viewers* everyday *objects* in quite different ways. Both eventually attracted a following. But like many artists before them, the op-art and pop-art painters had to educate their viewers.

**EXERCISE 63-2**    **Subjects**    To read about this topic, see section 63a in *Rules for Writers*, Sixth Edition.

A.  Each of the following sentences has three words or word groups italicized. One of these words or word groups is the subject. Find it and label it "S." Example:

          S<br>
**Many *artists* have *preferred* certain colors for their *work*.**

1.  During one *part* of his life, *Picasso* preferred the color *blue.*

2.  *There* are many famous *paintings* from *this* period.

3.  "*Blue*" refers not only to the predominant *color* of these paintings but also to their *mood.*

4.  In these paintings *you* will find *outcasts* or victims of *society* as the main characters.

5.  Do the *derelicts and beggars* in these pictures reflect *Picasso's* own sense of *isolation?*

B.  In the following paragraph, complete subjects have been italicized. Label the simple subject (or subjects) "SS." The first sentence has been done for you.

               SS                     SS

*Pierre-Auguste Renoir and his young friends* founded a new movement called "impression-ism." Instead of trying to reproduce a scene exactly, *impressionist painters like Renoir and his friends* blended small brushstrokes of different colors to give a general impression of a scene. Up close, *a careful observer of a restaurant scene* sees no solid edges on a table or a lady's hat, just small dabs of paint. At a distance, however, *that same careful observer* will see clearly the picture in the artist's mind. At first *the art world* laughed at and rejected the new movement. However, there is now *no serious argument about the importance of the impressionist movement.*

**EXERCISE 63-3     Direct objects and subject complements**     To read about this topic, see section 63b in *Rules for Writers,* Sixth Edition.

A.  Subjects and verbs have been labeled in the following sentences. Label each italicized word as a simple direct object (DO) or a simple subject complement (SC). Example:

                   s       v   *SC*
Pierre-Auguste Renoir's parents were *supportive* of their son's ambitions.

               s         v
1.  Renoir's love of art was *clear* to his parents.

         s  v               s     v
2.  When he was a *boy* of thirteen, they apprenticed *him* to a porcelain artist.

        s         v
3.  Renoir first learned the potter's *trade.*

         s   v
4.  Soon he was quite *skillful* at making and firing vases.

        s   v
5.  He enjoyed the *task* of decorating the vases even more.

B.  Using the pattern of each sentence as a model, write a short sentence of your own on any subject. Example:

S/V/SC: Renoir was an artist.

*Casey was a ballplayer.* _____  .

6.  S/V: Renoir studied.

    _____

7.  S/V: Renoir studied hard.

    _____

8.  S/V/SC: He became an excellent painter.

    _____

9.  S/V/SC: His paintings are cheerful.

    _____

10.  S/V/DO: Café owners liked his murals.

    _____

**EXERCISE 63-4    Indirect objects and object complements**    To read about this topic, see section 63b in *Rules for Writers,* Sixth Edition.

A. Subjects, verbs, and direct objects are labeled in the following sentences. Label each italicized word as a simple indirect object (IO) or a simple object complement (OC). Example:

         s      v   *IO*       DO
Renoir's parents gave *him* a good start in his chosen profession.

                         s         v             DO
1. Besides his parents, other people considered the young Renoir a fine *painter.*

   s       v                DO
2. He had shown local *businessmen* some of his work.

      s            v       DO
3. Owners of some Paris cafés gave *him* painting jobs.

   s  v    DO
4. He made the walls of their cafés *beautiful.*

       s     v                DO
5. The lovely scenes made both customers and owners *happy.*

B. Using the pattern of each sentence as a model, write a short sentence of your own on any subject. Example:

S/V/DO/OC: Renoir called his style of painting "impressionist."

*Casey called his style of batting "the best."* _____

6. S/V/IO/DO: Paris café owners offered Renoir much work.

_____

7. S/V/IO/DO: They gave him twenty orders for murals.

_____

8. S/V/DO/OC: They considered his work exceptional.

_____

9. S/V/DO/OC: People called him "the happy painter."

_____

10. S/V: His popularity increased.

_____

## EXERCISE 63-5   Direct objects, indirect objects, and object complements

To read about this topic, see section 63b in *Rules for Writers*, Sixth Edition.

---

Underline the verb of each sentence. Then label the complete direct object (DO) and any complete indirect objects (IO) or object complements (OC). Example:

```
        ┌─DO ┐              ┌──── DO────┐ ┌───── OC─────┐
Many people enjoy pop art. They find this new kind of art a refreshing change.
```

1.   During World War II, American mass media flooded London.

2.   The effect of that flood fascinated many London artists.

3.   Using the American material, British artists gave the world a new art form.

4.   To produce their art, the artists used images from popular culture.

5.   Someone named the new art "pop art."

6.   Most Americans find pop art very appealing.

7.   To some, it reflects the optimism of the 1960s.

8.   Items like flags, signs, and comic strips gave pop artists their subject matter.

9.   Artists like Jasper Johns and Roy Lichtenstein preceded the more famous Andy Warhol.

10.   Of all these artists, Andy Warhol best understood the media's power to affect people's thinking.

**EXERCISE 63-6**    **Pattern variations: Delayed subjects and understood subjects**    To read about this topic, see section 63c in *Rules for Writers*, Sixth Edition.

Underline the simple subjects in the following sentences. (Hint: These are tricky. The subjects are not always where you expect them. And you may even have to supply an understood *you*.) Examples:

> Have <u>you</u> ever heard of "color-field painting"?

*You* Read this exercise to find out something about it.

1. Making its appearance in the 1940s was a new kind of painting.

2. Was there any difficulty in explaining this new style?

3. No—look at paintings by Mark Rothko or Morris Louis for examples of this new color-field painting.

4. On their canvases are layers of color "washes."

5. What kinds of washes are they?

6. Among them are oil paints, inks, and acrylic.

7. Can colors all by themselves, with no "picture" of anything, make a painting?

8. Careful study of *Blue Veil* by Louis will reveal layer upon layer of different colors of acrylic, but no images.

9. There are many examples of color-field painting in art galleries today.

10. Visit a gallery to discover your own reaction to this kind of painting.

## EXERCISE 63-7    Pattern variations: Passive verbs    To read about this topic,
see section 63c in *Rules for Writers*, Sixth Edition.

In the following sentences, underline the verb twice and label it "VP" if it is passive. You should find six passive verbs. Example:

> ┌────── VP ──────┐
> Jasper Johns has often been called a pioneer of pop art.

1. Andy Warhol, a former commercial artist, was fascinated by everyday objects.

2. In his view, the beauty of everyday objects like soup cans was too often overlooked by people.

3. He was disturbed by America's casual attitude toward criminal executions and horrible accidents.

4. To make people aware of such things, he painted instead of writing or talking.

5. His silk-screened pictures of electric chairs speak for themselves.

6. His works have frequently been labeled "ironic" by art critics.

7. In his *Gold Marilyn Monroe*, Marilyn Monroe has been painted against a gold background, like an ancient religious icon.

8. Because of Warhol's clever use of pop-art technique, however, her image has been cheapened.

9. In the painting, Marilyn Monroe looks like a sleazy Virgin Mary.

10. By exercising his skill, Warhol succeeded in sending a message about American values.

**EXERCISE 63-8**     **Sentence patterns: Review**     To read about this topic, see section 63 in *Rules for Writers*, Sixth Edition.

Label the function of each italicized word or word group in the following paragraph. Use these codes: subject (S), verb (V), subject complement (SC), direct object (DO), indirect object (IO), and object complement (OC). The first sentence has been done for you.

        S            V     DO

*Renoir* definitely *had* firm *ideas* about work and about getting along with people. As for work, he believed that *people* everywhere *should use* their *hands* every day. He certainly did, and because he did, *friends* often *called* this hardworking *man* a *workman-painter.* Being called a workman-painter pleased Renoir. Work seemed to be more important to him than the finished product. "The only *reward* for work *is* the *work* itself," he said. He got along with people very well; even his enemies seemed to like him. When his opponents attacked his views, *he* frequently *responded* by suggesting a compromise. *He* freely *offered* other *people* his own successful *techniques* for getting along with his opponents. According to Renoir, *you* certainly *should give* your *enemies* a *chance.* You should also avoid a fight whenever possible. Why? If you avoid fights, your *enemies* often *will become* your *friends.* The *joy* in Renoir's paintings *might be explained* by these approaches to life.

**EXERCISE 64-1**     **Subordinate word groups: Preview**     To read about this topic, see section 64 in *Rules for Writers*, Sixth Edition.

In the following paragraphs, underline prepositional and verbal phrases once; underline subordinate clauses twice. The first sentence has been done for you; you should find fifteen phrases and five subordinate clauses. Answers to this exercise appear in the back of the book.

Louise Nevelson, who was once called "the finest living American artist," did not earn that title easily.

From her earliest years, she was artistically inclined. Drawing colorful pictures was a favorite childhood pastime. To decorate her room, she collected boxes of pretty rocks, shells, and fabric pieces. Encouraging her artistic interest, her family provided the independence that she needed.

Her husband, Charles Nevelson, who was a wealthy New York businessman, provided her with financial independence, but Louise Nevelson needed personal independence too. The marriage lasted for only eleven years. Then she and her son, Mike, went to her family home. Mike stayed there while his mother studied abroad. Studying, working, and making new friends, Louise developed the self-confidence to follow her own vision.

At times she must have wondered whether or not she had done the right thing. During Louise Nevelson's busiest and most exciting years, her paintings and sculptures were not popular with either the critics or the public. Later, however, her work won critical acclaim, and she was recognized throughout the art world. Rewarded and acclaimed, Louise Nevelson knew that she had made the right decision.

## EXERCISE 64-2    Prepositional phrases    To read about this topic, see section 64a

in *Rules for Writers*, Sixth Edition.

Underline the twenty prepositional phrases in the following sentences. Example:

**Children learn many things <u>from their parents</u>.**

1.  From her builder-father, Louise Nevelson learned an important tradition that had been handed down for generations.

2.  Like many other Jewish traditions, it is recorded in the Talmud.

3.  The Talmud is a book about Jewish history and laws; it is studied by Jewish scholars.

4.  According to the Talmud, Jews should always leave some part of a new house unfinished or unpainted.

5.  The unfinished part is there for a reason: It makes people remember the destruction of Jerusalem's Second Temple.

6.  As an adult, Louise moved into a dozen or more "new homes."

7.  Sometimes she abided by the tradition, but sometimes she forgot about it.

8.  Finally, she understood at last this tradition that had been handed down for all those years.

9.  She saw that over the years she had often left some work unfinished in her studio.

10. Both her work and her life were like her house: Only with an unfinished corner could they grow and change.

## EXERCISE 64-3    Subordinate clauses    To read about this topic, see section 64b
in *Rules for Writers*, Sixth Edition.

A.   Underline the subordinate clauses in the following sentences. Example:

**When Louise was part of a struggling young artists' group in New York, she met Diego Rivera.**

1.   Diego Rivera, who was a Mexican mural painter, introduced Louise Nevelson to other artists and their friends.

2.   One of the people whom she met, Marjorie Eaton, became her roommate.

3.   Louise also met Ben Shahn while she was working with Rivera.

4.   When Louise began working with Ben, she felt at ease with her art for the first time.

5.   She knew that she had found her niche.

B.   Identify each of the following word groups as a prepositional phrase or a subordinate clause. Example:

   a. After work                                    *prepositional phrase* _____

   b. After she had worked                          *subordinate clause* _____

6a. Before she went to class          _____

 b. Before her painting class         _____

7a. Since her happy childhood days    _____

 b. Since she had a happy childhood   _____

8a. Till the closing bell             _____

 b. Till the bell rang                _____

9a. After the mural was done          _____

 b. After the sculpture show          _____

10a. Until she mastered the skill     _____

 b. Until her first exhibition        _____

## EXERCISE 64-4     Prepositional and verbal phrases     To read about this topic,

see section 64a and 64c in *Rules for Writers*, Sixth Edition.

---

Some of the phrases in the following paragraphs are italicized. Label these phrases prepositional (PR), gerund (G), infinitive (I), or participial (PT). The first one has been done for you.

Louise Nevelson's first one-woman show came about because she was determined *to have her work recognized.* Her first choice of a showplace was the Nierendorf Gallery. *Exhibiting there* would put her in the same place where Picasso, Matisse, and Paul Klee had been exhibited. *Showing New York City's best modern art* had helped build a strong reputation for this gallery.

Nevelson went alone to the gallery. First she found Mr. Nierendorf, the gallery's manager. Then, *introducing herself quickly,* she stated quite simply that she wanted an exhibition in his gallery. He was surprised at her forthrightness, but he was also impressed. When he protested that he did not know her work, Nevelson simply invited him *to come and see it.*

He did—the next day—and he offered her a show in twenty-one days. *During the next weeks,* Nevelson got her pieces ready. When the show opened, it was Nierendorf's first exhibition *of an American artist.*

With a few exceptions, art critics liked the show. *Excited by her work,* one critic said that he would have "hailed these sculptural expressions as by surely a great figure among moderns"—if he had not found out the artist was a woman. That left-handed compliment did more harm to the critic than to the artist. Other critics, *seeing similar forms and rhythms,* compared her work favorably to Mayan work. Still others commented on the work's "wit" and "zest" and "interest in movement."

*Accepted very well,* the exhibition was extended past its closing time and gave Nevelson opportunities *to meet some important people*—but not a single piece of art was sold.

**EXERCISE 64-5**   **Verbal phrases**   To read about this topic, see section 64c in *Rules for Writers*, Sixth Edition.

The verbal phrase in each sentence has been italicized. Label these phrases gerund (G), participial (PT), or infinitive (I). Example:

>       *G*
> *Working with other artists* made Louise Nevelson very happy.

1. *Enjoying each other's company,* the members of Ben Shahn's artist group often ate dinner together.

2. Frequently, they would paint a picture right then and there *to celebrate their joy.*

3. *Needing the white tablecloth for their canvas,* the artists would push aside the dishes and food.

4. *Totally involved in their project,* they would look for "paint."

5. *Finding something to use for paint* was not usually a problem.

6. *Making paint from wine drops or pepper or anything else handy* gave them pleasure.

7. Each artist had a chance *to add to the picture.*

8. They enjoyed *adding details to the other artists' parts of the picture.*

9. *Relaxed and refreshed,* they would leave the restaurant content.

10. No one knows why the restaurant owner allowed them *to do this repeatedly to his table-cloths!*

**EXERCISE 64-6** **Subordinate word groups: Review** To read about this topic, see section 64 in *Rules for Writers*, Sixth Edition.

In the following paragraphs, underline prepositional and verbal phrases once; underline subordinate clauses twice. The first sentence has been done for you; you should find twenty more subordinate word groups.

Perhaps becoming a queen is one of every little girl's fantasies. During one experimental stage, Louise Nevelson gave herself that title. She called herself "Queen of the Black Black." While she was experimenting, she used only black materials in her artwork. She decided to make all her surroundings black also. Painting her walls black was the first step. Then she attacked the floors. She did not want to paint them; instead, she used stain to get the desired effect. Stained very dark, the floors did not reflect much light. Her work used no other color, and she insisted that black was "the total color."

At fifty-eight, Louise Nevelson was finally recognized. She became an artist who could expect regular exhibits, sales, and commissions. Museums and collectors bought her work eagerly, paying her well. She was awarded honorary degrees from various universities and accepted invitations to attend White House dinners. She enjoyed receiving these honors, but her greatest pleasure came later.

When Louise Nevelson celebrated her eightieth birthday, her hometown gave her what she had always wanted: The local museum exhibited her work, and the town bestowed a title upon her—"Queen of the City."

**EXERCISE 65-1**     **Sentence types: Preview**     To read about this topic, see section 65 in *Rules for Writers*, Sixth Edition.

In the following paragraphs indicate on the blank after each sentence whether the sentence is simple (S), compound (C), complex (CX), or compound-complex (CC). Two blanks have been filled in for you, and answers to this exercise appear in the back of the book.

Most Americans of any age recognize the name Jackie Robinson. _____ Even if they are not sports fans, Americans know some basic facts about him. _____ Jackie Robinson played baseball, he was good at it, and he was the first black man on a major league team. ___*C*___ Even more important than what Jackie Robinson did on the ball field is what he did off the field. _____

Several off-the-field incidents occurred when he was in the army during World War II. ___*CX*___ His sports prowess was well known, and he was avidly recruited for both football and baseball teams. _____ Because the football team was not integrated, Robinson re-fused to play on any army team. _____ While he was still in the army—and a second lieutenant to boot—the driver of the bus taking soldiers from the base into town ordered Robinson to go to the back of the bus. _____ (In those days in the southern states, the front and middle sections of a bus were for whites only.) _____ Robinson knew his rights as a soldier; when he refused to go to the back, he was arrested. _____ When his case came up, Robinson defended himself in the military court and won. _____

These off-the-field incidents foreshadowed important events that followed. _____

**EXERCISE 65-2**    **Sentence types**    To read about this topic, see section 65 in *Rules for Writers,* Sixth Edition.

A. In the following sentences, underline subordinate clauses. Then determine the sentence type and indicate it in the blank: simple, compound, complex, or compound-complex. Example:

**In 1945, Branch Rickey was president and general manager of the Brooklyn Dodgers.**

*simple* _____

1. Driven by his ambition to build America's strongest baseball team, Rickey wanted the best talent in the world. _____

2. Believing also that keeping nonwhites out of baseball was morally wrong, he had been studying the players in the Negro leagues. _____

3. He needed someone who was as good off the field as on the field. _____

4. The Negro leagues had plenty of good players, and Rickey's scouts watched them all, reporting on each one. _____

5. Impressed by the reports on Robinson's family life and by his postponement of marriage until he had a job, Rickey wanted to meet this ballplayer. _____

6. Reports also showed Robinson's fiery temper; worried, Rickey flew Robinson to New York for an interview. _____

7. In the interview, Rickey taunted Robinson with snide remarks and mean insults, making it quite clear that Robinson's ability to deal with such things—on and off the field—was as important as his ability to play ball. _____

8. Robinson understood: He could not lose his temper on the field or off, he could not respond in kind even if he was physically attacked, and he had to maintain this nonviolent stance for at least three years. _____

9. It was not a role that Robinson was used to; did he have the self-control to carry that role?

   _____

10. Robinson decided that he did, and the two men shook hands. _____

**EXERCISE 65-3**   **Sentence types: Review**   To read about this topic, see section 65 in *Rules for Writers,* Sixth Edition.

Indicate on the blank after each sentence in the following paragraphs whether the sentence is simple (S), compound (C), complex (CX), or compound-complex (CC). One of each kind has been filled in for you.

Robinson very quickly had a chance to test his commitment to non-violence; on the way to training camp in Florida, he and his bride were bumped from flights and refused service in the coffee shop. ___*C*___ When they finally got to Florida, they rode a segregated bus to get to Daytona Beach. _____ At training camp, white players stayed in nice hotels and ate in hotel dining rooms; Robinson and other blacks had to find homes or motels in the black community and eat in black restaurants. _____ Robinson kept his temper, diverting his anger into the force with which he handled the ball and bat. _____

The story best remembered about Jackie Robinson is probably the one involving Pee Wee Reese, a southerner on the team. ___*S*___ Some fans at a Cincinnati game yelled that he should not be playing with a black man, and Reese pretended not to hear. _____ He walked up to Robinson on first base, put a hand on his shoulder, and began a conversation. _____ Later, neither man could remember what they had talked about—but the fans understood Pee Wee's gesture and settled down. ___*CC*___

In his baseball career, Jackie Robinson broke many records and won many awards. _____ In 1962, he was inducted into the Baseball Hall of Fame—the first African American to be so recognized. _____ He was recognized outside the sports world as well, his top honor being the Presidential Medal of Freedom. _____ Again, what he did off the field was even more important than what he did on it. _____

Today, the Jackie Robinson Foundation provides education and opportunities for young people who, in turn, give back to the community. _____ Since its formation in 1973, it has sent into the world thousands of young people who commit to lifelong engagement in their own worlds, who understand the importance of their off-the-field lives. ___*CX*___

# Answers to
# Guided Practice and Preview Exercises

## EXERCISE 8-1 page 1

*Suggested revisions:*

Young slave Frederick Douglass enjoyed indulging in his favorite fantasy about slave owners. In his fantasy, everyone conspired against the slave owners. Slaves still in bondage gave no hint of an impending escape. Members of the community never revealed the whereabouts of escaped slaves. Slaves who escaped successfully never talked too much about how they got away. Recaptured slaves told their owners nothing at all. Even some white southerners who sympathized with the slaves gave no information to their slave-owning friends. Douglass enjoyed the final part of his fantasy the most. In it, Douglass imagined slave owners as being too afraid to hunt escaping slaves. The owners distrusted their slaves, their enemies, and even their friends.

## EXERCISE 9-1 page 5

*Suggested revisions:*

In his own time, one famous sixteenth-century man was known only by his given name, "Leonardo." Today he is still known by that single name. But then and now, that name suggests many different roles for its owner: biologist, botanist, inventor, engineer, strategist, researcher, and artist.

Sixteenth-century Venetian soldiers knew Leonardo as a military strategist. When the Turkish fleet was invading their country, Leonardo suggested conducting surprise underwater attacks and flooding the land that the Turkish army had to cross. Engineers knew him as the man who laid out new canals for the city of Milan. Scientists admired him not only for his precise anatomical drawings but also for his discovery that hardening of the arteries could cause death. To Milan's royal court, Leonardo was the artist who was painting impressive portraits, sculpting a bronze horse memorial to the house of Sforza, and at the same time working on a mural of the Last Supper.

Leonardo saw a three-dimensional s-curve in all of nature—the flow of water, the movements of animals, and the flight of birds. We recognize the same s-curve today in the spiraling form of DNA. Leonardo invented the wave theory: He saw that grain bending as the wind blew over it and water rippling from a stone cast into it were the same scientific event. It was as easy for him to see this wave in sound and light as to observe it in fields and streams. The math of his day could not explain all his theories, but twentieth-century scientists showed the world that Leonardo knew what he was talking about.

Leonardo saw very clearly that the powers of nature could be destructive and that human beings could be savage. At the same time, he saw a unity holding all life's varied parts together, a unity he could express in his art.

"Leonardo"—it's quite a name!

## EXERCISE 10-1 page 9

*Suggested revisions:*

Mary Wollstonecraft, an eighteenth-century writer, may have been England's first feminist. Her entire life reflected her belief in equal rights for women in all areas of their lives: personal, intellectual, and professional.

From childhood, she never had accepted and never would accept the idea that men were superior to women. As a young girl, she knew that her drinking and gambling father deserved less respect than her long-suffering mother. As an adult, she demanded that society give her the same freedom it gave to men.

Wollstonecraft also demanded that men pay attention to her ideas. She did not argue about an idea. Instead, she gave an example of what she objected to and invited her readers to think about it from various points of view. Working this way, she made few enemies among intellectuals. Indeed, she was attracted to and respected by some of the leading intellectuals of her day. Among them she was as well known on one side of the Atlantic as on the other. Tom Paine, the American orator and writer, probably knew her better than Samuel Johnson, the English writer, did.

Professionally, she was a governess, teacher, and writer. When her father's drinking destroyed the family, she and her sisters started a girls' school. Eventually, financial problems forced the school to close, but not before Mary had acquired enough firsthand experience to write *Thoughts on the Education of Daughters* (1786). As competent as or more competent than other writers of the day, she was a more persuasive advocate for women than most of them.

Modern feminists may find it ironic that current encyclopedia entries for "Wollstonecraft" refer researchers to "Godwin," her married name—where they will find an entry for her longer than the one for her famous husband, William Godwin.

## EXERCISE 11-1 page 13

*Suggested revisions:*

Sometimes it's hard to separate fact from fiction, to know what is history and what is folklore. Casey Jones, John Henry, Johnny Appleseed, Uncle Sam, Santa Claus—which of these were real men? We've been told stories about them all of our lives, but are those stories true?

There really was a railroad engineer people called "Casey" Jones; he got that nickname because of his birthplace, Cayce, Kentucky. There really was a "Cannonball" too; it was the Illinois-Central's fast mail train. And there really was a train wreck: Engine Number 382 rammed into some freight cars. The accident was not Casey's fault, and Casey died trying to save his passengers. When workers found his body in the wreckage, his hand was still on the air-brake lever. (Air brakes had recently been installed on trains to increase their braking power.)

John Henry was an African American railroad worker of great strength. In legend and song, he died after a timed contest against a steam drill. By using a hammer in each hand, he won the contest. John Henry drilled two holes seven feet deep; the steam drill bored only one nine-foot hole. The real John Henry died on the job too, crushed by rocks that fell from the ceiling of a railroad tunnel.

John Chapman, better known as Johnny Appleseed, was a wealthy and well-liked nurseryman who kept moving his place of business west as the frontier moved west. His boyhood friend Sam Wilson supplied meat to the US troops during the War of 1812. A worker told a government inspector that the "US" stamped on the meat stood for "Uncle Sam." Although it was a joke, it caught on, and Congress made the "Uncle Sam" identification official in the 1960s.

That leaves Santa Claus. As far as historians know now, Santa was not real. But legends say that there was once a man who . . .

## EXERCISE 12-1 page 17

*Suggested revisions:*

Hearing the name Karl Marx, people usually think first of Russia. Marx never lived in Russia at all. Actually, he spent almost all of his adult life in England. He was a political exile for the last half of his life.

Marx lived first in Germany. Born of Jewish parents, he completed his university studies with a PhD at the University of Jena. His favorite professor tried to get Marx an appointment to teach at the university. When that professor was fired, Marx gave up hope of teaching at Jena or any other German university. Because he was denied a university position, Marx had to earn his living as a journalist. He worked briefly as a newspaper editor in Germany.

Next came France, Belgium, and a return to Germany. First Marx and his new bride moved to Paris, where Marx worked for a radical journal and became friendly with Friedrich Engels. When the journal ceased publication, Marx moved to Brussels, Belgium, and then back to Cologne, Germany. He did not hold a regular job, so he tried desperately to earn at least enough money to feed his family.

After living in Paris and Brussels, Marx decided he would settle in London. He and his family lived in abject poverty while Marx earned what little income he could by writing for an American newspaper, the *New York Tribune*.

## EXERCISE 13-1 page 21

*Suggested revisions:*

Do you know how slavery began in America or how it ended? When the *Mayflower* landed in September 1620, slaves were already in America. A Dutch ship had unloaded and sold twenty Africans in Jamestown, Virginia, the year before.

Actually, slavery in America began long before that. Many early explorers brought slaves with them to the new land, and some historians claim that one of the men in Christopher Columbus's crew was a slave. From the 1500s to the 1800s, slave ships brought ten million African slaves across the ocean.

Most of the slaves stayed in Latin America and the West Indies, but the southern part of the United States received about 6 percent of them. Few northerners owned slaves, and opposition to slavery was evident by the time of the American Revolution. Rhode Island prohibited the importation of slaves even before the Revolutionary War. After the war, six northern states abolished slavery at once. Others passed laws to phase out slavery, and even Virginia enacted legislation encouraging slave owners to emancipate their slaves.

But it took a war, a tricky political situation, and a very clever former slave to free all slaves. History gives Lincoln the credit for liberating the slaves during the Civil War, and he deserves some credit, but emancipation was not his idea. Originally, no government officials seriously considered emancipation because they were so focused on winning the war to save the Union. Then an important black man talked to Lincoln and gave him the idea and the reason. This man said that freeing slaves would be good for the war effort and asked if Lincoln would agree to do it. Who was this man? He was Frederick Douglass, fugitive slave and newspaper editor.

## EXERCISE 14-1 page 25

*Suggested revisions:*

No one who knew Albert Einstein as a young child would ever have believed that he might one day be called the smartest man in the world. None of his teachers could have predicted success for him. A shy, slow learner, Albert always got into trouble in class. He consistently failed the subjects he did not like. His family could not have predicted his success either. Albert could not even get to meals on time. Night after night his parents had to postpone dinner until servants searched the house and grounds and found the boy. He would be full of apologies but have no explanation to offer for his lateness except that he was "thinking." Once his angry father dangled his big gold watch at Albert and told him to figure out how late he was. Albert, who could not tell time, was fascinated by the tiny magnetic compass hanging from the watch chain. The boy asked so many questions about the compass that he did not eat much dinner anyway. When Albert begged his father to lend him the compass to sleep with, his father let him borrow it. Years later Einstein wondered whether that little compass had been the beginning of his interest in science.

## EXERCISE 15-1 page 29

*Suggested revisions:*

Everyone has heard of Martin Luther King Jr. After studying for the ministry at Boston University and earning a doctorate in theology, he went home to the South to work as a minister. He started working in civil rights and became the most influential leader of that cause in America. When he died, the victim of an assassin's bullet, his name was almost synonymous with "civil rights." Historians and biographers have recorded his leadership in the fight to gain basic civil rights for all Americans. Many people who know of his civil rights work, however, are not aware of his skill as a writer. In addition to his carefully crafted and emotional speeches, King produced other important writing.

Among King's most famous writings is his "Letter from Birmingham Jail." Written to answer a statement published by eight Alabama ministers that King's work was "unwise and untimely," the letter shows King to be a man who had great patience with his critics. Eager to get these ministers to accept his point of view, King reminds them that they are ministers. Their goodwill, he says, should help them see that his views hold value. Instead of attacking them personally, he analyzes their arguments and then presents his own views. Does he use many of the emotional appeals for which he is justly famous? No, in this letter King depends on logic and reasoning as the tools to win his argument.

## EXERCISE 16-1 page 33

*Suggested revisions:*

Adam Smith, the founder of modern economics, proposed a theory in the eighteenth century that has made him controversial ever since. This economist, born in Scotland and educated in England, wrote the first complete study of political economy. *The Wealth of Nations* was published in the same year that Americans declared their independence from England—1776. Smith's book pointed out the interdependence of freedom and order, economic processes, and free-trade laws. Although Smith's thinking did not really affect economic policies significantly during his lifetime, its influence in the next century was considerable. Among economists, "the invisible hand" and "laissez-faire" are synonymous with Smith's name. History has only made Smith's ideas more controversial. Say "Adam Smith" to conservative businesspeople, and they will smile and respond with words like "He was a good man—really understood how business works!" Say "Adam Smith" to liberal reformers, and they will grimace and mutter something like "He was an evil man—really sold the average citizen down the river." Both of these reactions are extreme, but such responses indicate that the controversy aroused by Smith's ideas is still alive.

## EXERCISE 17-1 page 37

*Suggested revisions:*

A. In the 1800s, an Englishman named Thomas Robert Malthus became involved in economics. He was very interested in predicting how many more people would populate the world eventually and how much food would be available for them. What he figured out was frightening. He said people kept having children faster than society could produce enough to feed them. There was no way to avoid it. Hard times and wars would kill most people. According to Malthus, famine, plagues, and even wars were necessary to eliminate some excess people so the remainder could have enough food.

B. Robert Malthus proved that population grows faster than food supplies. His thinking led him to oppose any help for poor people. He believed that by relieving the immediate problems of the poor, the government actually made it harder for people to feed their families. Malthus said that if the government subsidized their basic needs, people would only have more children, thus increasing the population even more. Then the inevitable famine or drought would have to eliminate even more people to help a few survive. Everyone from worker to supervisor was caught in the same predicament. It is no wonder that when the English historian Thomas Carlyle finished reading Malthus's theories, he pronounced economics "the dismal science."

**EXERCISE 18-1** page 41

*Suggested revisions:*

Economics is not totally dominated by men. Even in the 1800s, when Thomas Malthus and David Ricardo were the experts, one leading writer about economics was a woman, Jane Marcet. Marcet wrote for the popular press. One of her favorite topics to write about was political economy. In her book *Conversations in Political Economy,* Marcet summarized economic doctrines before 1800. Her aim was different from that of either Malthus or Ricardo. Rather than propounding a new theory of her own, she popularized theories of other people. Twentieth-century women have done more than write about theories that men have proposed. Some of them have taken the initiative to develop their own ideas. Sally Herbert Frankel, for example, made the first official calculations of the Union of South Africa's national income. She is only one of the increasing number of women who make careers in economics.

**EXERCISE 19-1** page 47

*Suggested revisions:*

Four young Englishmen added a word to the world's vocabulary in the 1960s, a word that became synonymous with the 1960s, especially with the music of that time. That word was, of course, "Beatles." The Beatles became the most famous popular musical group of the twentieth century and held the loyalty of many fans into the next century.

The Beatles were popular in Liverpool, England, and in Hamburg, Germany, before they came to America on tour and became world famous. Liverpool and Hamburg loved the four young men and their music. The Beatles' favorite club was the Cavern in Liverpool, where they hung out together, played day and night, and attracted many fans. A Liverpool disc jockey first called attention to them, and a Liverpool music critic and record store owner became their first manager. The disc jockey called them "fantastic," saying that they had "resurrected original rock 'n' roll." The music critic who became their manager, Brian Epstein, made them shape up as a group. Promoting them, arranging club dates for them, and badgering record companies for them, he was determined to win a recording contract for this exciting new group.

In England, the record buying led to the publicity. In America, the publicity led to the record buying. Everyone wanted copies of the original singles: "Love Me Do," "Please, Please Me," and "From Me to You." In America, audiences made so much noise that no one could hear the music. Crowds of screaming teenagers surrounded the Beatles wherever they went, determined to touch one or more of these famous music makers. Reporters observing the conduct of fans at Beatles' concerts found that they had to invent another word to describe the wild, almost insane behavior of the fans. They called it "Beatlemania."

**EXERCISE 20-1** page 53

*Suggested revisions:*

Have you ever heard of the Wobblies? Not many people have these days. That's a shame, because they did at least two things for which they should be remembered. They probably saved the labor movement in America, and they definitely gave American folk music some of its most unforgettable songs. No one really knows how they got their nickname, but almost everyone knows a song or two that they inspired.

The Wobblies were the members of the Industrial Workers of the World (IWW), a small but militant coalition of radical labor groups. The Wobblies could not get along with the major union groups of the day; in fact, they alienated most of those groups.

Although the major unions disliked the Wobblies immensely, they learned some valuable lessons from them. The first lesson was to avoid getting involved in politics. If there was one thing the Wobblies hated more than capitalism, it was politics. The Wobblies avoided politics for one good reason: They [*or* they] believed that political affiliation caused the death of unions. What else did the major

unions learn? They learned to deal realistically with workers' problems. Major unions also learned new recruiting techniques from the Wobblies. In addition, they copied the Wobblies in devoting their energy to nuts-and-bolts issues affecting the workers.

The major unions never recognized their debt to the Wobblies, but the debt was still there for historians to see. When historians began to compile the story of American labor unions, they finally recognized the contributions of the Wobblies.

**EXERCISE 21-1** page 60

convey, are, are, are, has, is, seem, enjoy, is, is

**EXERCISE 22-1** page 64

*Suggested revisions:*

Everyone has heard of Dorothy and Toto and their tornado "flight" from Kansas to Oz. Everyone also knows that the Oz adventure was pure fantasy and that it ended happily. But another girl from Kansas took real flights all around the real world. Whenever she landed safely after setting one of her many records, everyone rejoiced and sent congratulations to her. When she disappeared on her last flight, the whole world mourned. Not every pilot can claim to have that kind of following.

Neighbors knew that Amelia Earhart would not be a typical "lady." A child as curious, daring, and self-confident as Amelia was bound to stand out among peers. When she and her sister Muriel were young, girls were supposed to play with dolls. If girls played baseball or collected worms, they were called "tomboys" and were often punished. Boys and girls even had different kinds of sleds—the girls' sleds were lightweight, impossible-to-steer box sleds.

But the Earhart family lived by its own rules. Amelia's father, whom she depended on for approval, bought Amelia the boys' sled she longed for. Many fast trips down steep hills gave Amelia a foretaste of flying with the wind in her face.

The closest Amelia came to flying was on a homemade roller coaster. She and her friends built it, using an old woodshed for the base of the ride. They started eight feet off the ground and tried to sled down the slope without falling off. No one was successful on the first attempt, but Amelia kept trying until she had a successful ride. Satisfied at last, she declared that the ride had felt "just like flying."

**EXERCISE 23-1** page 68

*Suggested revisions:*

George and Mary Jones lived in Memphis during the Civil War. They were sympathetic to the Union, but the city definitely favored the Confederates. Being caught in the middle made the war years especially hard on them. They looked forward to a much better life after the war.

At first, it seemed that they were going to have that better life. George got a job as a labor organizer, and Mary stayed at home to care for their four healthy children. Then came yellow fever. In nine months, Mary went from a happy wife and mother to a despondent widow who had no children. She had to find work. Because a person must have some meaning for living, she needed work that she could care strongly about.

By 1900, Mary had become involved in union activities all over the United States. She found her calling among the coal miners and their wives, a calling she followed for the next thirty years. Making friends with workers and outwitting private detectives, she held secret meetings to help the miners organize and plan strategy. The newspaper often reported her ability to outwit and outlast mine bosses and lawyers as well as to reawaken courage in disconsolate workers.

Mary Jones spent many nights in jail, but often her jailers did not know what to do with this attractive gray-haired woman whom the workers called "Mother." The jailers' confusion simply amused Mary, who was far more used to jail than her jailers could imagine.

## EXERCISE 24-1        page 72

They, them, We, her, They, them, they, he, president's, she


## EXERCISE 25-1        page 76

whom, whom, Who, whoever, whom
[*Note:* The *whom* in the last sentence may be dropped.]


## EXERCISE 26-1        page 80

Novelists have often used their storytelling talents to influence people's thinking. Charles Dickens did it in nineteenth-century England. From *David Copperfield* to *Oliver Twist*, book after book depicted the plight of the poor and other really unfortunate members of society. Harriet Beecher Stowe did it in nineteenth-century America, but with hardly as many books. Her *Uncle Tom's Cabin* depicted slavery so well that the book strongly influenced antislavery sentiments in the decade before the Civil War.

Harriet Beecher Stowe considered slavery sinful and wanted her book to help end slavery quickly and peacefully. People first read parts of the novel ten years before the beginning of the war. An abolitionist magazine published it a few chapters at a time, hoping the effect of the story would make readers feel so bad about slavery that they would rally to the abolitionist cause. Many people, reading *Uncle Tom's Cabin* installment by installment, did become convinced that nothing could be worse than living in slavery on a southern plantation.

None of the abolitionists, who devoted their energy to abolishing slavery, expected a perfect world when the book itself was published in 1852. But they certainly hoped that the book would be influential. It was. Of all the novels published that year, it was the best-seller on both sides of the Atlantic. Its popularity was good news for the abolitionists. Harriet Beecher Stowe's wish came true.


## EXERCISE 27-1        page 84

*Suggested revisions:*

Most Americans today don't realize that the American democratic system did not always include African Americans and women. The constitutional amendments passed after the Civil War granted former slaves and all native-born African American men full voting rights, but the new amendments ignored women. Women had to wait much longer—more than half a century—to be given the right to vote.

Some individual states allowed women to vote as early as 1900, but by 1910 women activists decided to focus their energy on a federal amendment. When Woodrow Wilson became president in 1913, women demonstrated along the inauguration route, marching and holding signs demanding the vote for women. Then in 1917, Alice Paul and a militant faction of the suffrage movement picketed the White House and even chained themselves to fences. When they were threatened and attacked by male mobs, police ignored the men and arrested the women. In prison, the women endured filthy cells, force-feeding when they went on a hunger strike, and ill treatment. Some women were restrained for many hours in uncomfortable positions with their arms high over their heads. One angry official repeatedly asked a doctor to declare one or more of the women insane. (The doctor refused.)

President Wilson was a man with major problems—a war abroad and women fighting for their rights at home. At first he tolerated the women picketers; he even sent coffee out to them. Then he just wanted the women to lay down their signs and banners and go home. But the increasing pressure from moderate and radical voices in the movement as well as public outrage over the women's prison treatment finally forced Wilson to support a constitutional amendment for women's voting rights.


## EXERCISE 27-5        page 88

*Suggested revisions:*

Almost everyone has heard about Aesop's fables, but most people know very little about Aesop himself. Most of what we know about Aesop is a mixture of hearsay and conjecture. We do know that he was a slave in Greece. One theory is that before he came to Greece he had lived in Ethiopia for most of his life and that "Aesop" is a much-shortened form of "the Ethiopian."

Aesop was not a storyteller then, though he would have loved to speak well enough to tell a good story. He stuttered so badly that he did not even try to talk. In one story we learn, however, that he could communicate. A neighbor brought a gift of figs to Aesop's master. Greatly pleased, the master planned to enjoy the figs after his bath and directed that they be put in a cool place until he was ready. While the master was bathing, the overseer and his friends ate the figs. When the master discovered the loss of his figs, the other slaves placed the blame on Aesop. They knew that if Aesop were able to speak, he could defend himself, but they did not fear this stammering slave.

The master ordered that Aesop be flogged. Aesop got the master to delay punishment briefly. Aesop drank a glass of warm water, ran his fingers down his throat, and vomited only water. Pointing at the overseer, he made gestures that the overseer and his friends should do as he had done. They drank the water, ran their fingers down their throats—and vomited figs.

Although Aesop's cleverness saved him from a flogging, it also made an enemy of the overseer. Aesop discovered a basic truth about life: Being right doesn't always help one to make friends.


## EXERCISE 28-1        page 93

*Suggested revisions:*

Immigrants have come to the United States from all over the world. Initially, new settlers were mostly European, Irish, or English. By the twentieth century, many Asians had taken the frightening boat trip across the Pacific. Usually the men came first. After they had made enough money for passage, their wives and children were brought over. All thought that if they worked hard, they would make a good life, as earlier European immigrants had done. Unable to live comfortably in their homelands, a large number of Chinese and Japanese settled in the western part of the United States.

These new immigrants worked on the railroads and in the mines. American businesses recruited Chinese labor because American workers would not accept the wages that were paid. Why did workers decide to come to America anyway? Somehow the idea got started that America was a "golden mountain," where people could pick up gold nuggets after an easy climb. Once they got here, most immigrants worked hard because they hoped to make enough money to bring relatives over to America too.

Before and during World War II, many Germans who had been persecuted by Hitler escaped to America. After the war, thousands of "displaced persons" were welcomed by the United States. Later, refugees from Asia, Africa, Latin America, and the Caribbean wanted to be accepted. Franklin D. Roosevelt once said, "All of our people all over the country, except the pure-blooded Indians, are immigrants or descendants of immigrants." If Roosevelt were alive today, he would know that his statement is still true.


## EXERCISE 29-1        page 102

*Suggested revisions:*

People all over the world have stories that are part of their culture. Many cultures have a creation story that explains how the world came to be. Sometimes the story tells how a single piece of the world got its characteristics. It is not surprising that these stories exist; what is surprising is how similar the stories are. Consider the Cinderella story, for example. Cinderella has different names in different places, and details of her adventure are not the same; but the basic story echoes around the world.

In Egypt, she is called Rhodopis (the word means "rosy cheeked"). Rhodopis is a Greek slave in an Egyptian home. She does not have eyes or hair like anyone else in the home. Her green eyes look quite different from the eyes of the other girls. Their dark, straight hair almost never gets tangled; her yellow, curly hair blows into a tangled mass around her face. Her light-skinned face turns red and burns when she is in the sun too long. When someone calls her "Rosy Rhodopis," she blushes, and her cheeks became even rosier.

Unable to make friends with the other girls, Rhodopis turns to the animals in the nearby woods and streams.

## EXERCISE 30/31-1 page 106

*Suggested revisions:*

A descendant of one of those earliest immigrants to North America played a pivotal role in helping later Americans explore their country. There were tribes of American Indians living all over what is now the United States. Each tribe had its own language and customs. Some tribes raided others and took prisoners who then became the raiding tribes' slaves. That is what happened to a young Shoshone girl now known as Sacagawea.

This girl, like many young girls, had a nickname, "He-toe." "He-toe" was the sound a local bird made, and the girl's movements were so swift that friends thought she resembled that bird. When a raiding party of Hidatsas easily captured this young girl, they named her Sacagawea—"bird woman." Sacagawea was about twelve years old. The frightened young girl did not try to escape but accepted her role and worked for her captors. After [*or* In] a few months, she had acquired a reputation for good sense and good work.

The tribe married Sacagawea to a white man, Toussaint Charbonneau; she was his second wife. Soon pregnant, this typical Indian wife did the chores and left all decisions to her husband; but inwardly, she longed to explore new places and meet new people. She may have been controlled by her husband, but she never missed a chance to learn whatever she could.

When white men appeared, many Indians were curious. Sacagawea had never seen a man with yellow hair—or red hair. Nor had she ever seen a black man. All these men were trying to get to the "Big Water" far to the west. They would have to cross mountains that they had not even seen yet. They needed horses and guides that the Shoshones could supply and an interpreter who could speak the Shoshone language. Imagine their surprise when this interpreter, whom they had hoped to find, turned out to be a woman—an attractive young Shoshone woman.

## EXERCISE 32/33-1 page 115

If a boy wanted to join the football team at Carlisle Indian School, he had to go through a difficult test. Any boy who wanted to be on the team had to stand at one of the goal lines; all the first-string players stood around the field. When the ball was punted to the new boy, he had to catch it and try to get all the way to the other end zone with it. The team members tried to stop him before he could get very far. Only a few players had ever gotten as far as the fifty-yard line, so "Pop" Warner, coach at the Carlisle Indian School, considered it a good test.

One day a quiet Indian boy surprised Pop. The boy caught the ball, started running, wheeled away from the first players who tried to stop him, shook off the others, and ran the ball all the way to the opposite goal line. Convinced that the player's success was an accident, the coach ordered him to run the play again. Brusquely, the coach spoke to the players and reminded them that this workout was supposed to be tackling practice. Jim, the nineteen-year-old six-footer, simply said, "Nobody tackles Jim." Then he ran the ball to the goal line a second time.

Well, almost no one tackled Jim Thorpe successfully for many years. Life itself got him down and made him fumble more often than his football opponents did, but he was usually able to recover and go on. The first blow was the death of his twin brother while the two boys were still in grade school. This tragedy was followed by others; by the time Jim was twenty-five, he had lost his brother, his mother, and his father to death. They left him a Native American heritage: His father was half Irish and half Native American, and his mother was the granddaughter of a famous Indian warrior named Chief Black Hawk.

Fortunately or unfortunately, along with his Native American heritage came great pride and stoicism. That pride kept him silent when the greatest blow of all came: He was forced to return the Olympic medals he had won in 1912 because he was declared to be not an amateur. He dealt stoically with his personal tragedies. When infantile paralysis struck his son, Jim Thorpe disappeared for a few days to deal with the tragedy alone. His stoicism also saw him through a demotion to the minor leagues and sad years of unemployment and poverty before his death.

Even death's tackle may not have been totally successful: After Jim Thorpe's death, his Olympic medals were returned, and a town was named after him.

## EXERCISE 34-1 page 123

When Cheryl Toussaint came in second in a race she had never planned to run, she started on a road that led to the Olympics and a world record.

Cheryl began running almost by accident one day when she went to watch a city-sponsored track meet in Brooklyn, New York. During the preliminaries, the officials announced an "open" race; it was one that anyone could enter. Cheryl wanted to enter, but she was dressed in a skirt and sandals. Four things made her run: One friend traded shoes with her, another let her borrow jeans, several called her "chicken" if she didn't run, and one girl dared her to run. Coming in second in that race led this teenager to many places, including Munich, Germany; Toronto, Canada; and Montreal, Canada.

There were, however, many races to run and lessons to learn. Cheryl joined the all-female Atoms Track Club, and she began training under Coach Fred Thompson. Like most coaches, Fred had his own way of testing newcomers. He watched a new runner carefully; however, he gave her no special attention. Instead, he just gave her orders one after another. He would tell Cheryl to run laps, go through exercises, and do practice starts; at the same time he would never comment on how she performed. If the newcomer endured the hard, time-consuming workouts without encouragement or praise, Thompson was sure that she was ready for real coaching.

Cheryl quit after two months; for six more months she stayed out. During that time she thought about her attitude toward work, her poor record at school, her pleasure in running, and her lack of goals. When she returned, Thompson welcomed her back. Coach Thompson knew how special Cheryl was. He not only convinced her she was college material but pushed her to achieve the highest goal of the amateur athlete—the Olympics.

## EXERCISE 35-1 page 127

In 1951, Althea Gibson broke the color barrier in women's tennis and became admired all over the world. No one who knew her as a teenager would have predicted her success. By the time Althea Gibson reached her teens, her record showed three indications of trouble: running away from home, dropping out of school, and losing the one job she had been able to find. To survive in her neighborhood, Althea depended on a small welfare allowance, occasional handouts, and plain old luck. She listed her skills as the following: good bowler, great two-on-two basketball player, and fast paddleball player. Even after she began playing tennis and moving in upper-class Harlem society, she resented the efforts of the society ladies to improve her. They busied themselves with tasks such as correcting her manners and restricting her behavior. Looking back, she later summed up her attitude: She [*or* she] said she wasn't ready to study about "how to be a fine lady." At eighteen, she finally got a waitress job, a congenial roommate, and a good friend.

## EXERCISE 36-1 page 131

During the 1990 troubles in Panama, American television and newspaper reporters had an exciting piece of news. They reported that for the first time American female soldiers had been engaged in actual combat. Acting as her soldiers' leader, Captain Linda Bray led her troops into combat. Names of two additional women who were involved in combat, Staff Sergeant April Hanley and PFC Christina Proctor, were reported in the newspapers. Theirs were the only names reported, although other women also took part.

It wasn't the first time an American woman had fought in an American battle, but it's not likely that many people are aware of that fact. The Civil War had its female fighters too. Loreta Janeta Velazquez fought for the Confederates in the Civil War after her husband's death. Like many other women whose husbands were killed in that war, she must have asked herself, "Who's going to take his place in battle?" The decision to fight was hers alone. Someone is sure to ask how that was possible, even in those days. Military identification was not very sophisticated in the 1860s. Someone's willingness to fight was that person's major qualification, and each fighting unit needed to replace its losses as fast as possible. Velazquez simply disguised herself in men's clothing, found a troop needing replacements, and joined the fight. Loreta Janeta Velazquez was Linda Bray's Civil War predecessor.

## EXERCISE 37-1                                        page 135

1. The doctor answered, "You can do nothing but pray."
2. When the bandages were removed and the shades were opened to let in the bright sunlight, the doctor asked, "What do you see?"
3. "Nothing," said the boy. "I see nothing."
4. The village priest said, "I have recently seen a remarkable school." He had just returned from a trip to Paris.
5. "In this school," he added, "blind students are taught to read."
6. "You didn't say 'read,' did you?" asked the boy's father.
7. The boy responded to the priest's words as if they were a trick of some kind: "Now you are joking with me. How can such a thing be possible?"
8. The boy, Louis, thought it would be great fun to visit that school someday.
9. His father promised, "We will go soon, Louis."
10. And so it happened that ten-year-old Louis Braille entered the National Institute for Blind Youths and began the long effort to erase the fear people had of even the word "blind" [or blind].

## EXERCISE 38-1                                        page 139

After Louis Braille invented his new system that would allow blind people to read and write, he tested it thoroughly. Students and faculty of the National Institute for Blind Youths were excited at how easily they could master it and encouraged Louis to demonstrate the system to the French educational authorities, who made the rules for the institute. Louis agreed to do so.

When Louis held the demonstration, all went well. What excitement he and his friends felt! But the authorities would not recommend that the institute adopt Louis's new system. Why didn't the French authorities recognize the advantages of Braille's system? Did they have a vested interest in the old system of teaching the blind? Or a real doubt about the system? Whatever their reasons, they delayed the pleasures of reading for thousands of people. In addition, a new director, Dr. Pignier, even outlawed the use of the system at the institute for four years.

Although unhappy and disheartened, Braille never gave up; he knew his system would enable the blind to read.

## EXERCISE 39-1                                        page 144

The most famous woman in America is Miss Liberty—a 450,000-pound, 154-foot resident of New York City. For people all over the world, the Statue of Liberty symbolizes America. Yet the idea for the statue came not from America, England, or even New York itself—but from France. Three men can claim the credit for construction of Miss Liberty: (1) Frédéric-Auguste Bartholdi, sculptor; (2) Alexandre-Gustave Eiffel, structural engineer; and (3) Richard Morris Hunt, architect. France gave the statue to the United States, and the United States provided the pedestal on which it stands.

Two Americans contributed significantly to the statue. The first was Joseph Pulitzer, then owner and publisher of the *New York World* and a Russian immigrant. He led several fundraising efforts and urged every American to give what he or she could to help build the pedestal. The second American who contributed significantly was Emma Lazarus. She wrote the famous lines on the bronze plaque inside the statue. Her three-word title "The New Colossus" (huge statue) alludes to a statue built in the harbor of Rhodes in ancient Greece. The most quoted lines from "The New Colossus" are probably these: "Give me your tired, your poor, /Your huddled masses yearning to breathe free."

## EXERCISE 40/41/42-1                                  page 149

Everyone has heard of Christopher Columbus, but not many people know much about him. Most people learn that he discovered America in AD 1492. Some people know that he had three ships, and they might be able to name them. (The ships were the *Niña*, the *Pinta*, and the *Santa María*.) A few people might even remember that Columbus thought he had found the Indies. And those with great self-confidence might be willing to guess at the number of trips he made to his India. (It was four.) Probably no one could tell you his favorite word, *adelante*.

If they were asked what Columbus was trying to prove with his expensive journey, most people would reply that he was trying to prove the world is round. They would be wrong. If they were asked what Columbus meant by "the Indies," they would probably say "India." They would be wrong again. If they were asked what Columbus's rank was, they would probably say "captain." They would be wrong again. If they were asked what his sailors feared most, a number of them would reply, "They feared that the boats would fall off the edge of the earth." And they would be wrong again.

Isn't it strange that people can be so ignorant about a well-known man like Columbus?

## EXERCISE 43/44/45-1                                  page 153

Columbus's return to Spain from his first exploration was difficult. The *Niña* and the *Pinta* were separated, the *Niña* almost sank, and the governor on the island of Santa María put Columbus's whole crew in jail. It seemed a miracle that both boats arrived in the harbor at Palos on the same day.

As difficult as that return was, the reception at court quite made up for it. Columbus certainly made an all-out effort to impress the court, the city, and the entire country. Lavishly attired, he received a grand welcome as he led his entourage into Barcelona, the Spanish capital. It must have been a sight to behold: a procession like none Barcelona had ever seen before. Leading the parade was a gaudily bedecked horse carrying Columbus, followed by six captive "Indians" and all the crew. Everyone but Columbus was carrying boxes, baskets, and cages full of interesting and exotic items.

When the group reached the throne room, King Ferdinand and Queen Isabella stood up to greet Columbus formally and admire his apron-covered captives. Columbus asked the royal couple to accept gifts of plants, shells, darts, thread, and gold. As intrigued as they were with the other gifts, King Ferdinand and Queen Isabella basically wanted gold. Luckily, Columbus had collected enough samples of it to satisfy them.

By the end of the first week home, Columbus had such prestige that everyone wanted to accommodate the wishes of the Italian sailor at the court of Spain. Columbus had no doubt that he would receive a commission for a second voyage of exploration or even colonization.

## EXERCISE 62-1                                        page 159

readers, N; are, MV; of, P; its, ADJ *or* PN; and, C; or, C; formal, ADJ; starts, MV; simply, ADV; with, P; should, HV; everyone, PN; about, P; certain, ADJ; when, C; them, PN; acts, MV; government, N; bold, ADJ; been, HV

## EXERCISE 63-1                                        page 168

group, S; had, V; problem, DO; they, S; went, V; They, S; gave, V; paintings, IO; bursts, DO; lovers, S; were surprised, V; artists, S;

made, V; scenes, DO; bright, OC; would pour, V; sunshine, S; Were, V; paintings, S; bright, SC; cheerful, SC; painters, S; are admired, V; forms, S; are, V; examples, SC; Both, S; showed, V; viewers, IO; objects, DO

Subordinate clauses: that she needed; who was a wealthy New York businessman; while his mother studied abroad; whether or not she had done the right thing; that she had made the right decision

**EXERCISE 64-1** page 176

Verbal phrases: Drawing colorful pictures; To decorate her room; Encouraging her artistic interest; Studying, working, and making new friends; to follow her own vision; Rewarded and acclaimed
Prepositional phrases: From her earliest years; of pretty rocks, shells, and fabric pieces; with financial independence; for only eleven years; to her family home; At times; During Louise Nevelson's busiest and most exciting years; with either the critics or the public; throughout the art world

**EXERCISE 65-1** page 182

Simple; Complex: Even if they are not sports fans (subordinate clause); Complex: what Jackie Robinson did on the ball field, what he did off the field (subordinate clauses); Simple; Complex: Because the football team was not integrated (subordinate clause); Complex: While he was still in the army—and a second lieutenant to boot (subordinate clause); Simple; Compound-complex: when he refused to go back (subordinate clause); Complex: When his case came up (subordinate clause); Complex: that followed (subordinate clause)